– THE ART OF CREATIVE –
PRUNING

– THE ART OF CREATIVE –
PRUNING

Inventive Ideas for Training and Shaping Trees and Shrubs

JAKE HOBSON

TIMBER PRESS
Portland · London

To our boy, Digby

Frontispiece: 'Bunch of grapes' *tamazukuri*, California style.
Photo by Brian Eden.

All photographs are by the author unless otherwise stated.
All illustrations by Marjorie C. Leggitt.

Published in 2011 by Timber Press, Inc.

The Haseltine Building
133 S.W. Second Avenue, Suite 450
Portland, Oregon 97204-3527
www.timberpress.com

2 The Quadrant
135 Salusbury Road
London NW6 6RJ
www.timberpress.co.uk

ISBN-13: 978-1-60469-114-6

Library of Congress Cataloging-in-Publication Data

Hobson, Jake.
 The art of creative pruning : inventive ideas for training and
shaping trees and shrubs / Jake Hobson. — 1st ed.
    p. cm.
 Includes bibliographical references and index.
 ISBN 978-1-60469-114-6
1. Topiary work. 2. Pruning. I. Title. II. Title: How to train and
shape trees and shrubs.
 SB463.H63 2011
 715'.1—dc22   2011007954

Printed in China

A catalogue record for this book is also available from the
British Library.

CONTENTS

PREFACE
On Rock and Roll, Pruning and Love

I ONCE READ AN ARTICLE about the musician Lou Reed, who was looking back on his Velvet Underground days. I remember reading that he still gets a buzz every time he turns on his amplifier and feels the hum of electricity flow through his guitar. This made quite an impression on me—since the beginning of his musical career, Lou has probably turned on his amp most days, and it was inspiring to read that each time he does, he feels the same excitement, the same potential of what the day might bring, as he did when he was a teenager.

Granted, pruning is not quite rock and roll, but I get a similar feeling to that guitar amp buzz that Lou described every time I reach for my pruning tools at the beginning of the day. The anticipation of the damp morning dew soaking my shirt sleeves, the sweet smell of fresh box, or boxwood, clippings, the sun—or rain—on my back and the satisfying first clip of the day through to the inevitable aches and blisters that will arrive later that evening.

I love the physical action of pruning, in all its manifestations. I love climbing up ladders and chopping things down. I love the quick jobs that only take five minutes but achieve so much, and the satisfied feeling at the end of a demanding job well done. Most of all I love the results: the effect that a few deliberate cuts, or years and years of gradual teasing can have, not just on a plant, but the whole garden. I love the way pruning can create landscapes, evoke far off places and memories and how it can surprise and even shock, focusing and distracting

viewers by turns. I love its solidity and permanence, but also its fragility and the grey area it occupies between man and nature, gardener and garden.

What qualifies as creative topiary or decorative pruning? Anything really, when approached from the right direction and with the right mindset, but I get particularly excited by interesting forms, ambitious scale, unusual plant types (not so much exotic as unexpected) surprising contexts, breathtaking locations, visible enthusiasm on the part of the owner or creator and a generally vibrant atmosphere. Gardens in Provence, France, tend to score heavily when it comes to location—Gourdon, hanging onto a cliff face suspended over a rocky valley, is one such spectacular example, while the Keage water treatment plant in Kyoto, Japan, although clearly not the most glamorous place in the world, does have the most amazing repetition of azalea blobs planted on its banks, the sheer weight of numbers there achieving a look that more sophisticated gardens could not.

Where do I draw the line? There is no room in this book for animal topiary—no teddy bears or squirrels allowed, although since writing this, I have noticed that one or two examples seem to have somehow crept in. If that upsets you, write your own book. On the other hand, although pruning itself is not weighed down with creative potential, I rank agricultural hedge flailing—the cutting of farmland hedgerows by tractors armed with lethal flailing chains as practised in the UK—as a highly sculptural process that is fully worthy of inclusion in this book. Some people disapprove of this method for environmental reasons, but the sight of a well-flailed

OPPOSITE: **Chaos at Marqueyssac. Photo by Jean Laugery, courtesy of Marqueyssac gardens.**

hedge running across the countryside is as inspirational to me as any garden I have seen. If you still feel any doubt about the possibilities and potential of agricultural pruning, as opposed to horticultural pruning, look no further than the tea plantations in the Far East, where bizarre landscapes of tea cover entire valleys like limestone pavements.

During the creation of this book, I have become much more aware of how interconnected the various genres of pruning I was thinking about actually are. When I began writing, I started off with a very clearly defined list of chapters and sub-sections. It soon became clear, however, that it was not chapters that were called for, but some sort of family tree, or a map of a river system with endless tributaries, flood plains, backwaters and oxbow lakes—or even some vast web of interconnected strands. A Venn diagram of pruning turns into one large circle that encompasses everything and excludes nothing, so please forgive any apparently erratic subdivisions and understand the dilemmas I faced in writing this book. Eventually I settled on chapters covering topiary and shaping, cloud pruning and organic topiary, hedges, *niwaki* and Japanese-influenced pruning, decorative tree pruning and a slightly indulgent look at creative pruning.

A brief note on my use of Japanese: to my mind, written Japanese, when romanised, reads better without the commonly accepted Hepburn system of transliteration, so I don't use macrons over the o and u vowels when extended, nor do I add an extra o or u in place of the macron. Only very occasionally does this simplification cause problems, but most of time I believe it makes for a far more pleasant read.

....

OPPOSITE, TOP: **Gourdon, Provence, France. Photo by Peter Edwards.**
OPPOSITE, BOTTOM: **Tea plantations in India. Photo by David Davis.**
BELOW: **Keage water treatment plant, Kyoto, Japan. Photo by Jeffrey Friedl.**

ONE
Topiary and Shaping

THIS BOOK IS NOT ABOUT TOPIARY, not in the normal sense. It is about where topiary lies within the fields of pruning and shaping in general, and where it could go. Topiary, as most people understand it, is the clipping of trees and shrubs—woody plants, as they are known in this context—into shapes. The shapes can be simple geometric ones such as balls, cones, pyramids and cubes; they can be more elaborate affairs, multi-tiered wedding cakes for example; or they can be playful animal shapes or faces. That is the Western view of topiary, but when looking to the East, and to Japan in particular, one sees a lot of shaping of trees and shrubs that looks rather different. Once we are alert to new possibilities, they start popping up closer to home too, and all of a sudden the term topiary can imply far more than one might expect.

Rather than focusing on the classic topiary gardens of Europe and the United States, I find it more interesting to focus on the smaller, more recent additions to the genre. In France, Marqueyssac and Sericourt are late twentieth century creations that are privately owned and packed to the brim with exciting topiary, while in the UK the gardens at West Dean College have been gradually clipped and sculpted into shape under the watchful eye of head gardener Jim Buckland. In North America, meanwhile, Pearl Fryar's remarkable garden in South Carolina stands out as being something rather unique. The notion of topiary as being formal or old-fashioned is firmly dealt with in these gardens—each one is lively, fresh and involving, a far cry from the stereotype.

....

OPPOSITE: **The bastion at Marqueyssac.**

MARQUEYSSAC
As if another reason was needed to visit the Dordogne in south west France, the owners of the gardens at Marqueyssac in Vezac have been busy restoring—or reinterpreting—this fantastic chateau garden. Its baroque muddle of box (*Buxus sempervirens*) topiary has graced the cover of many topiary publications, and I felt before visiting that I would find it predictable, possibly even a disappointment due to its familiarity. Luckily for me, my autumnal visit proved me wrong.

I had arranged to arrive early, hoping to avoid the crowds and bright sunlight that make photography so challenging. My crowd avoidance tactics were certainly successful—the gardens were deserted and shrouded in a heavy mist until ten o'clock, making photography difficult (I never think to bring a tripod with me) but creating a beautifully moody, poetic atmosphere that revealed mysterious huddles of box shapes as I approached them.

This alternative take on the traditional parterre and knot garden (the low, symmetrical patterns of hedges traditionally seen in French gardens, such as Versailles) is in part a restoration of the original garden. Pictures of the garden in its former state before work began in 1996 are on show, when the box was overgrown and the layout sometimes unrecognizable. In places, the original planting has been preserved—the box dates back to when Julian de Cerval inherited the property in 1861 and introduced his love of Italian plants—but there has also been a tremendous amount of new planting since the restoration, filling in gaps and planting new areas from scratch.

The English-language leaflet for the gardens says of the box plants: "They form a strict network, imposing themselves on the entire estate like the bearers of order, the principle directors of a nature ruled over by unruly ways." Box is very much the theme, and only from above, from the higher terraces, is it really possible to define the layout and to imagine what the original design might have looked like.

Within the main terraces, the bastion's individual shapes can be discerned within the mayhem: the odd spiral punctuates the horizon, a row of Russian dolls flank a path, the outline of a stringed instrument, perhaps a lute, is tucked away in a vast pillow as if resting in its own velvet-lined case, accompanied by quavers—both semis and demis—and fragments of obscure Eastern and Arabic scripts. One area has a field of formal lollypop standards poking out from flat slabs of pedestal below, the bleached white trunks linking the tops to the bottom, giving the impression of mature trees standing in parkland.

I asked Stephanie Angleys, the lecturer at Marqueyssac, where the inspiration for the restoration stemmed from, and the answer was, predictably, a variety of sources: the Italianate combination of architecture and landscape (the terraces have a definite Mediterranean feel to them, despite being nearer the Atlantic coast than the Mediterranean, helped by the odd *Cupressus sempervirens* dotted about the bastion); the Napoleonic style of rolling, sinuous lines; Romantic nineteenth-century gardens; Japanese gardens (and in particular azalea *karikomi*) and, crucially, the landscape of the Dordogne—the valleys and hills that surround Marqueyssac.

As a first-time visitor to the area, I was particularly struck by the connection with the local landscape, from the general feel of things right down to the small details. This area of the Dordogne is well known for its walnut production; all over the countryside are neat rows of walnut trees and our breakfast that morning consisted not only of fresh walnuts, but walnut cake too. It struck me that the nut, in all its brainy intensity, could well

have been an inspiration for this garden—the flowing, organic formations, the tucks and clefts, the apparent chaos, and even, if you will allow me a passing poetic fancy, something about the taste, the sweet but bitter dryness of the nut.

Wandering from the main terraces, the garden unfolds along the rocky spur behind. In the shade of scrubby holm oaks (*Quercus ilex*) more box grows, some clipped into low hedges marking the paths, some into blobs and other forms of semi-formal topiary. The rest are allowed to grow naturally as big shaggy things, which in the shade never quite make it to tree status, but out in the open, where their growth is more concentrated, they remind one of what a box plant can achieve in 150 years, as given time and suitable conditions, *Buxus sempervirens* grows into quite a serious little tree. Further along the spur are the makings of a box tunnel, an avenue of box that flanks the path and has been allowed to grow tall (and thin) and is being encouraged to join at the top, with a little help from some twine.

A clearing in the scrub reveals a striking collection of large box balls, arranged in an abstract formation with a multi-stemmed oak beyond. In contrast to the intensity of the main terraces, this seemed to offer some calm, some respite, and in the atmospheric mist of the early morning formed one of my strongest memories of the garden.

So where does Marqueyssac fit in? How does it compare to the billowing cloud pruned yew hedges in the UK? Can it be compared to the *karikomi* gardens of Japan? (These days it is hard not to refer to Japan whenever one sees billowing, organic blobs—the Japanese are, after all, the masters of azalea clipping.) Or should it be judged more in the Mediterranean tradition? Comparisons are largely irrelevant of course—the garden is fantastic and unique. Its setting, scale, quality and depth

PAGE 12: **Marqueyssac in the early morning mist.**
PAGE 13: **Box tunnel.**
OPPOSITE: **Multi-stemmed oaks and box.**

of the topiary and the emotions it encourages are like no other. Children love it too, treating the low level box more like a playground than a garden, while the peacocks that strut around the bastion and the mountain goats that block the remote paths along the spur add an exotic, wild and slightly surreal feel to the place.

Amazingly, all the clipping here is done by hand. The main terraces that are out in the sun get two clips a year, once in early summer and then again in the autumn, while the less formal, shadier and thus slower growing areas get one clip. The place was immaculate when I visited, and clearly always is, thanks to the work of head gardener Jean Lemoussu and his team.

Box boxes

Marqueyssac is a good example of a particular form of topiary that has become popular in contemporary gardens, and seems particularly widespread on the European continent. Square or cubed topiary, normally seen grown in box (giving rise to the lovely notion of box boxes) pops up randomly all over the place. Marqueyssac has an impressive slope of tumbling dice, known as Chaos, seen here cascading down towards the cafe area, resembling a cubist landscape painting and quite in contrast to the rest of the garden. Jacques Wirtz's garden in Schoten, Belgium, has batches of cubes, rectangles and plinths tucked away behind the cloud hedges, the strong lines of the shapes creating a great interplay with the organic lines of the hedge.

These cubes owe much to the forms of modernist architecture. They offer up all sorts of possibilities, the flat planes and horizontal lines creating bold shapes that add dynamism and energy when used amongst more natural planting or rounded balls and blobs. In the André Citroën Park in Paris, squared box is used in a thoroughly contemporary setting, planted as a labyrinth of slightly varying heights within a solid block, reminding me somewhat of the layout of a circuit board. It also suggests urban planning and tower blocks, while the clean white trunks of birches that spring up from within confirm the urban, modernist concept.

Personally, I find the constant use of white-barked birches in contemporary gardens and landscapes to be boring, unimaginative and long past its sell-by date, no doubt thought up by unimaginative, desk-bound designers. It seems they are used as the default tree in virtually every urban design project, as if the design software the designers use has built-in planting lists within its program. Please, if anyone is still listening, we know they are pretty and modern looking, but how about something different next time?

The danger of box boxes or any square topiary, including hedges, is that it is very hard to get them, and keep them, looking good. The best hedges are those that swell out slightly at the bottom, so light reaches their entire height and the bottom is as dense and healthy as the top. For a cube to be a cube (and not have a wider base than top, which would make it some sort of trapezoid) the sides must, of course, be vertical, and here the modernist gardener faces a conundrum: they want the perfect cube, but the perfect cube will never be perfect, at least not for long, because the bottom rarely gets enough light and will inevitably get thin and straggly—not what modernism is about at all.

When it comes to pruning, the tops grow far more vigorously than the sides, and getting the edges nice and sharp when there is not enough new growth to clip is a real skill. I would always use shears rather than mechanical hedge cutters for this kind of work—preferably long-handled ones that reach to the ground without you having to bend too low. Hedge cutters tend to gloss over irregularities, hiding previous errors rather than correcting them, while shears allow the time and precision to iron them out.

OPPOSITE, TOP: **Chaos at Marqueyssac.** Photo by Jean Laugery, courtesy of Marqueyssac gardens.
OPPOSITE, BOTTOM: **Box cubes and domes at Jacques Wirtz's garden in Schoten, Belgium.**

Solutions to the problem of the perfect cube involve either cheating (making your cubes slightly wider at the bottom, so they get enough light) or giving the cube as much light as possible by not overcrowding it. I am glad to say that the maintenance team at the André Citroën Park have not resorted to cheating—modernists never cheat—but thanks to the design, there is not enough light for the individual plants to thrive. Some of them look decidedly ropey, even the outward-facing ones. Ultimately, the best way to approach cubes is to enjoy the good bits (the tops) and ignore the bad bits (the bottoms). In Paris, they have made the most of the varied horizontal planes, planting them close enough together that one tends not to notice what is going on lower down.

SERICOURT

The garden at Sericourt in Northern France is an altogether different experience to Marqueyssac, although equally ambitious. Started in 1985 by owner Yves Gosse de Gorre, it is a collection of informal rooms, a rose tunnel, a grass labyrinth, a woodland area, a hazel walk and stacks of topiary in all shapes and sizes. Whereas at Marqueyssac there is no hiding from the topiary, Sericourt offers some respite—this is a garden with a lot of topiary, rather than a true topiary garden.

The geometric garden, with its open expanse of lawn containing box-edged beds and other random geometric arrangements of box, looks to the formal modernism of Jacques Wirtz in Belgium, while the topiary garden is given over entirely to a path flanked on both sides by a smorgasbord of cones, domes, balls, spirals and cubes, giving a master class in random arrangement.

The yellow garden is an ornamental twirl of variegated yellow box in a clear gravel area, contained within a low circular box hedge. The motif escapes out of the circular enclosure and spills out on to the grass beyond, like a yin and yang parterre gone wild. The contrast of the variegated and green box, the grey gravel and the green of the grass creates an interesting pattern full of movement and energy.

The most startling part of the garden has to be the fastigiate yew columns (*Taxus baccata* 'Fastigiata Aureomarginata') that stand in ranks on either side of another stretch of lawn, in the warrior garden. They remind me of the basalt rock formations at the Giant's Causeway in Northern Ireland, with their irregular heights and almost octagonal appearance. Massed topiary of any kind, and that of repeated shapes in particular, has a presence that seems to be so much more than the sum of its parts—the repetition, the partly concealed characters lurking at the back, the effects of light and shade adding depth—it all adds up to a stunning sculptural landscape.

From a topiary point of view, Sericourt really stands out thanks to its variation and the surprises it offers. Any one of its different rooms would be an ample achievement for most enthusiasts, but at every turn, the next room offers a new approach to topiary. If there were any danger of the whole thing being too serious, there is a more playful element to the garden too: tables and chairs of yew and a motley gang of thugs, part Easter Island, part Elisabeth Frink's sculpted bronze heads, which have been cut into low, rounded conifers. Heavy of brow and slightly ridiculous, they stare out from their huddle like ranks of helmeted soldiers waiting for their orders.

There are, of course, countless other gardens on the Continent that are full of topiary and shaped plants, each with their owners' personality stamped on them and all worthy of inclusion, but one which I only learned about very recently is Priona in The Netherlands, largely

OPPOSITE, TOP: **The yellow garden at Sericourt.** Photo by Yves Gosse de Gorre.
OPPOSITE, BOTTOM, LEFT: **The topiary garden at Sericourt.** Photo by Yves Gosse de Gorre.
OPPOSITE, BOTTOM, RIGHT: **André Citroën Park, Paris.** Photo by Laura Knosp.

PAGE 20, TOP: **Yew furniture at Sericourt.** Photo by Yves Gosse de Gorre.

PAGE 20, BOTTOM: **Hired thugs in the garden at Sericourt.** Photo by Yves Gosse de Gorre.

PAGE 21: **Fastigiate yews (*Taxus baccata* 'Fastigiata Aureomarginata') in the warrior garden at Sericourt.** Photo by Yves Gosse de Gorre.

THIS PAGE: **Clipped box at Priona, summer and autumn.** Photos by Beatrice Krehl.

the work of Dutch gardener Henk Gerritsen. He had a unique approach to gardening, involving tolerating weeds and pests as natural ingredients in the garden and celebrating the natural cycle of life and death. I never had the chance to visit one of his gardens, but clipped box and yew were a common theme of his work. This was sometimes seen to be at odds with his use of and attitude towards wildflowers but, just as with Japanese *karikomi*, the shapes he created were as natural and organic as could be, like herds of seals frolicking on the beach. Herbaceous plants and weeds were allowed to grow around them and die back over the winter, giving the feel of moss-covered boulders in an enchanted forest.

WEST DEAN

West Dean College, tucked into the South Downs in West Sussex, is a fascinating place for keen gardeners to visit, especially for eager pruners. Both the restored walled gardens, which are full of fantastic examples of fruit training and pruning, and the gardens around the house are well worth a visit. Owned by The Edward James Foundation, the grounds had been slipping gently into disrepair for much of the twentieth century, and it took the destruction of the great storm of 1987 to inspire a turnaround. Four years later Jim Buckland and his wife, Sarah Wain, arrived and got stuck in.

There is not much traditional, formal topiary at West Dean, although there is a yew hedge with rather nice low crenellations, or battlements, cut into it and a set of fine mushroom-shaped yew puddings and cubes in front of the house. Jim describes these as being the precedent for the rest of the garden. Inspired by these shapes, clipping became the unifying theme linking the various disparate elements of the garden. Certainly over the ten years or so that I have known West Dean, more and more of it has become clipped and shaped.

OPPOSITE: **Organic topiary on a large scale at West Dean.**

Everywhere one looks, there are beds of once over-grown evergreens that have been gradually turned into sculptural landscapes. Enormous laurels (*Prunus laurocerasus*) that were allowed to grow unchecked for too long have been cut back and reshaped into flowing mounds that link the garden with the surrounding landscape. While the underlying intention might have been to unify the garden as a whole, this approach to shaping is the perfect practical solution for overgrown evergreens in general—once the hard work of cutting back is over, all they need is a yearly clip with long reach hedge trimmers to keep them in shape.

An old evergreen hedge has had a similar treatment, turning it into a billowing piece of organic topiary on a scale so vast that a cherry picker is needed to reach the top half. It is made up of evergreen holm oak (very commonly planted in this part of Sussex), yew and holly. Although it is clipped into a smoothly flowing form, one can make out the individual species within the hedge, with the different textures and colours emphasizing the surface tension. The overall effect is similar to gazing at woodland from the outside—within one continuous outline a variety of species and shapes and dark spaces are visible, all combining to form a homogenous, heaving mass.

Closer to the house are two blobberies—groups of blobs—one of yew, the other box. Like all good blobberies, they are made up of irregular shapes and sizes, their dynamics shifting as one moves around them. Seen from the side, the yews spew out of the corner of the house like some organic, living being. When seen from different angles, the same shapes make bold, varying silhouettes of interlocking forms against backdrop of the Downs. There is also a fine example of a multi-stemmed *Osmanthus ×burkwoodii* here, for those with an eye for such things. The second, more recently planted blobbery, winds alongside a stone path neatly framed by flint walls, essentially forming a cloud pruned box hedge, but one that is low and deliberate, rather than monstrous and random.

Repetition, repetition

With its many clipped shapes, West Dean is a fine exponent of the art of repetition. Using the same or similar shapes over and over again in a garden adds to the overall coherence of a place, defining it and giving it added presence—one impressive yew pudding in the garden would soon be forgotten, but a dozen of them remain etched in the memory. A row of box balls, a group of blobs—any particular shape used over and over creates a sculptural presence that is more than the sum of its parts, creating a perspective and depth that directly engages the viewer. Japanese gardens do a similar thing with their use of *karikomi* and pines, and so do British churchyards, though perhaps more unwittingly in the latter case, with their simple palette of yew.

PEARL FRYAR'S TOPIARY GARDEN

Pearl Fryar's garden in Bishopville, South Carolina, U.S.A., is one of the most surprising topiary experiences I have ever come across. Started in 1981, from a determination to win the local Yard of the Month competition, it is one man's extraordinary labour of love, packed full of weird and wonderful abstract topiary. With no gardening or pruning experience, Pearl set about clipping and shaping the trees and shrubs one by one, and gradually developed a reputation for his work, to the point where he is now recognized as an important figure in the self-taught artist and folk art world, the subject of books and television shows.

The story goes that at one point Pearl was given some books on European topiary by an impressed visitor to his garden, but he soon discarded them, deciding that he had nothing to learn from the established traditions, preferring to continue working instinctively, as he had done so far. Much of his topiary has a unique character to it, in particular the large junipers that appear to grow in a gravity-free zone, with their branches trained

OPPOSITE: **Pearl Fryar's garden in South Carolina, U.S.A.** Photos by Nic Barlow.

26

up, down, around and in on themselves. Similar at first glance to Californian-style Japanese pruning, these trees are more chaotic, with gaping holes and bare branches. They really are like nothing else I have seen.

As well as in the garden itself, Pearl's work and enthusiasm for topiary has spread through the entire town of Bishopville. The local Waffle House has a spiral and cubes of juniper outside (in return for free meals for Pearl), as does the John Deere franchise, while Pearl's neighbours in his street have joined the party too, giving the town a topiary theme that it has now become well known for. This social element of the topiary links it to the folk art movement and gives the garden extra dimensions, those of educator and uniter.

MAKING TOPIARY

Growing your own topiary, on any scale in any kind of garden, is a relatively long-term project, but the rewards are endless. These days, of course, it can all be bought ready-grown—at a cost, but without the challenge, fun, satisfaction and personal touch that comes with the Do-It-Yourself, or Grow-It-Yourself, approach. The basic forms of the ball, cone, spiral, wedding cake and formal standard covered here can lead one on to more ambitious projects, which will only be limited by your imagination and determination. Recognizing everyday shapes and forms and coming up with suitable names for the various shapes you invent is all part of the fun.

Balls and blobs

The box ball, the most basic form of topiary, also happens to be one of the hardest to get right. Perfect spheres are nigh on impossible, but once a degree of compromise has been reached, the process is fairly straightforward. Plant them in pots or in the ground (a much better long-term choice) and arrange them formally, symmetrically or in a free-form manner like the Japanese do. I refer to box (*Buxus sempervirens*), the most common material for this sort of treatment, but other small-leaved evergreens such as evergreen azaleas and yew will do a similar job.

Whether intended to be as close to spherical as possible, or more of a blobby mushroom shape, the formative process is the same—start with a young plant either grown from a cutting or bought for hedging—typically 6 in. (15 cm) tall and 3 in. (7–8 cm) wide.

Mushrooms and blobs (the terms are interchangeable, although technically of course mushrooms have stems, so can also be standards) are easier than spheres, as with box balls there is a danger of the fully round shape either becoming slightly pointed at the top, or heading towards mushroom-like flatness. Beware of cutting flat planes around the plant, rather than a nice round shape—the trick is to keep moving and never dwell too long on one spot. To get a good finish, I find it helps to get down to the same level as the plant, so you are looking at it, not down onto it. If you have trouble getting clean outlines, imagine you are a lathe-like machine that is set on automatic, and cut to an invisible outline. In some places, you will take more foliage off, in others you might barely touch it, or even clip through thin air, but this helps to iron out any irregularities and in time will give a much better outline. It is a good idea to put a pruning sheet around plants to catch the clippings, especially when you are working on gravel. In my enthusiasm, I often forget to.

Once the shape is established, clip box once after the growth flush (in the UK, the traditional day to clip is Derby Day, in early June). The temptation is always to clip sooner, but it really is worth holding out or else you will find the plant grows in irregular spurts over the summer and ends up looking messy by autumn. By the end of summer, smaller box plants will need a second clip, but larger, less vigorous ones can often get by with just the one. Use hedge shears for larger projects and one-handed clippers for more detailed areas. Take care to tidy up the bottom of the ball as well as the top, as the

HOW TO MAKE A BOX BALL OR MUSHROOM

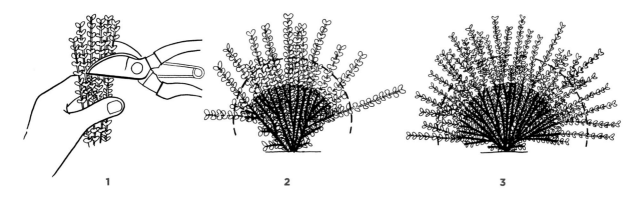

1   **2**   **3**

1. Grab the top of the plant in one hand, bunching up the foliage. With secateurs (pruners) or topiary clippers, make one clean cut across the top, removing around an inch of growth from the top of the plant, to encourage side growth.

2. In the plant's second year of growth, use topiary clippers to prune the plant into a well-rounded, nearly spherical shape for a box ball. If you are creating a mushroom, remove more growth from the top of the

plant, making the plant wider than it is high. Also try to avoid cutting any horizontally inclined growth, as this will take longer to grow back.

3. Repeat each year, following the previous year's pruning pattern, in late spring/early summer.

....

BELOW: **Clipping an established box ball.**
OPPOSITE: **Use one-handed topiary clippers for fine details.**

surface tension of its resting point is vital to the overall look, and a scruffy undercarriage can ruin the overall outline just as easily as a scruffy top. Some plants that are deep within summer borders are best left untouched until the autumn, when their herbaceous neighbours have died down around them, after which the box can come into its own over the winter. Ultimately it depends on the individual gardener and their levels of fastidiousness and time available: some prefer the shaggy look while others go for the crisp, just-clipped style, pruning several times over the summer.

Wedding cakes, cones, pyramids, spirals and standards

Wedding cakes, cones, pyramids, and spirals all start their lives in a similar fashion. Box is ideal for smaller shapes, while yew, bay (*Laurus nobilis*) and many other species are suitable for larger scale projects. The key to all these shapes is a single, fairly straight, leader. Bushy, multi-stemmed plants might look promising at the start, but as they grow they will become unpredictable, swelling in all the wrong places. To ensure a good leader, it is worth using a bamboo cane as a support down the middle of the plant, to strengthen the leader while you are removing any competing branches. Nowhere is this more essential than for the wedding cake tier, where so much of the main trunk is visible.

WEDDING CAKES: To grow a multi-tiered wedding cake, or *étager*, start off with a single leadered plant and have a good think about your intended scale. Once you start a project like this, certain decisions become final. How tall will it be? How many tiers? Wide or narrow tiers? Ones that are wide at the bottom but narrow towards the top? As an example, imagine a (quite imposing) finished product that is about 10 ft. (3 m) tall, with equal spacing of the trunk and cake parts in 12 in.

....

OPPOSITE: **Wonky wedding cake at Levens Hall, Cumbria.**

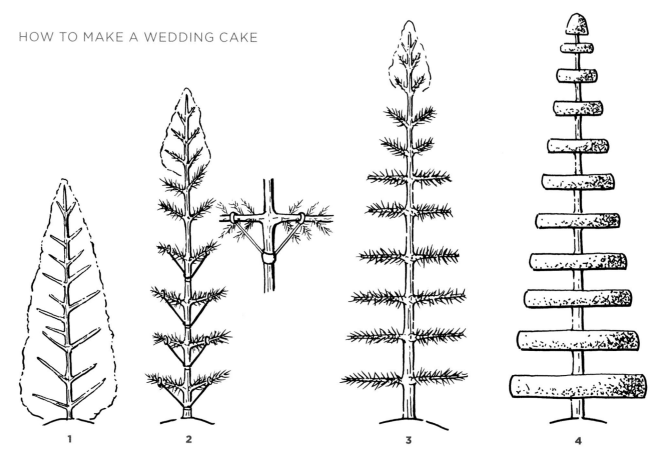

1   2   3   4

1. Establish where the first tier will be by looking for a good set of side branches that are between 1 and 2 ft. (30–60 cm) off the ground and are spread evenly around the trunk.

2. Remove all other branches below this point, and within the next 12 in. (30 cm) above it. Then continue removing unwanted branches, using the next group of side branches to become the second tier, and so on. Train the branches down with string to create a flat plane, if desired.

3. As each tier fills out its area, clip the edges and top to make a flat, slab shape, and tidy up each tier's undercarriage too.

4. It is particularly important to keep the foliage level and even near the top of the cake, where you will see the undersides and the gaps as much as the tops of each slab.

More ideas for wonky wedding cakes

OPPOSITE: **Yew *étager* wedding cake** at Levens Hall, Cumbria.

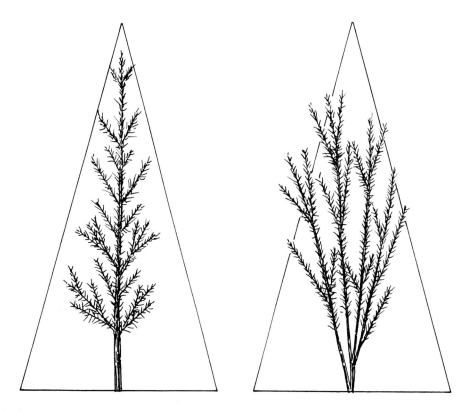

Single-stemmed plants are a better choice than multi-stemmed ones for pyramids and cones

(30 cm) sections. The cake should taper in at the top, which not only looks good, but also allows light into the lower branches. As the tree grows, each new tier will announce itself, with the lower tiers slowly becoming more established. For a 10 ft (3 m) plant, aim for a diameter of around 4 ft. (1.2 m) at the bottom, tapering up to 8 in. (20 cm) or so at the top—although these measurements are purely a guide and the final ones are, of course, entirely up to you.

The importance of the single, straight trunk will prove itself very quickly, as the overall effect should be as formal and symmetrical as possible. In some old topiary gardens like Levens Hall however, one sometimes comes across wonky wedding cakes that appear to be more like the ramps of multi-storey car parks that have lost their shape over time and have developed a character all their own.

CONES AND PYRAMIDS: Growing a cone or pyramid involves a similar start to that of the wedding cake. A single leader is absolutely essential here, because a cone or a pyramid should narrow as it gets taller, but a trunk that branches halfway up is liable to bulge and swell at just the wrong point.

However, as the trunk is hidden, it need not be totally straight—the odd kink is not a problem. If starting off with a young plant, firstly cane the leader and with a pair of shears quickly rough off the edges of the plant, treating cones and pyramids in exactly the same way at this point, as they share the same basic form. In future years, tie in the leader to the cane to ensure a straight trunk, and start clipping the sides into shape. For pyramids, as their volume starts to develop, think about the four sides, including which way they will face and how steep you would like their angles to be. Clipping small

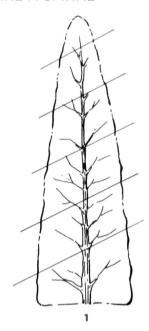

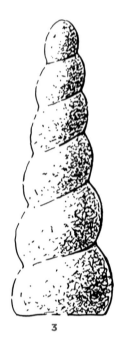

1. Rough out a spiral shape on your plant with a pair of topiary clippers and some string, if desired. Try to keep the gradient of the spiral equal the whole way up, but also think about making the swirl bigger at the bottom and slowly reducing its size towards the top.

2. Using secateurs or shears, cut in along the spiral, removing any small branches that do not contribute to the spiral.

3. As the plant develops, aim to finish the top of the plant directly in the centre, with a round-nosed point or tip.

cones and pyramids is best done from directly above, with the plant between your legs. Larger plants need to be approached from above and below, but watch out for Womble Nose Syndrome (wombles, if you remember, have big pointy noses that tend to bulge slightly halfway down). The tendency is to clip the bottom of the plant with the shears aimed downwards, and then the top of the plant from below, and inevitably there is a break in fluidity of your clipping that can result in a swollen midriff, resulting in womble-nosed plants.

SPIRALS: Creating a spiral uses a combination of the cone and wedding cake techniques. A great way to start is with a ready-grown cone, although you can of course start with a young plant, in which case a single, straight leader is called for. Using an established cone, some people suggest wrapping a length of string around it, spiraling up from the bottom, to give a guiding line to cut to. This is a good way to get started, although not absolutely necessary.

Over the following years, you can decide if you want round, shell-like spirals or flat-edged ones like a spiral parking ramp. Not all spirals are true to their name—some suggest the general movement without always spiraling completely up and around the whole plant. This is fine when only seen from one angle, in a border for instance, but when seen from all sides, their weaknesses are exposed.

STANDARDS: The formal standard, whether full, meaning with a clear stem typically up to 6 ft. (1.8 m), half, with a clear stem up to 3–4 ft. (90–120 cm) or even

Ball, mushroom, onion and cube standards

mini, with a shorter trunk of no more than 2 ft (60 cm) is a great launching point for all sorts of variations on the standard theme. The classic lollipop can easily mutate into a standard mushroom, onion or even a cube, and the formula for producing them is all pretty much the same until the final clipping stage. Evergreens are the obvious candidates—yew, box, bay and Portuguese laurel (*Prunus lusitanica*) are the traditional European choices, but by no means exclusively so—most evergreens and many conifers are suitable material too, as are deciduous trees and shrubs. *Robinia pseudoacacia* is one such example, although these are less common than evergreens. In California, the olive (*Olea europea*) is a popular choice, as is *Ficus microcarpa* and other tender evergreens, such as *Cinnamomum camphora*.

The foundations of a good formal standard lie in its trunk—get a good trunk and the rest is plain sailing. If buying ready-made trees, whether full or half standard or at some point in between, be sure to select good, straight trunks with no kinks. If you do get a dud, try turning the plant 45 degrees and hiding the problem—out of sight, out of mind. If starting from scratch and training your own trunk, be ever vigilant with a pair of secateurs and bamboo cane, straightening the leader and removing any competitors at an early stage.

The basic approach to growing a formal standard is ensuring the trunk is straight, and then pruning at the right height to build up the crown. This involves cutting out the leader to encourage branching, or with more established plants, cutting into the trunk itself. Ideally, make the cut at a set of side branches, but if that is not possible, cutting at a bare section of stem or trunk should produce a good flush of growth that will make the foundations of the crown the following year. Shaping the head is much the same as forming a ball shape, only on a stick: regular cutting back to consolidate, followed by clipping into shape.

Lollipops should be as spherical as possible, mushrooms can have flat bottoms, while onions and liberty caps have a Moorish nipple on top. Size-wise, half standards are easier to produce and clip than full standards—the moment you need a ladder to reach the top, it not only slows you down, but also prevents you from getting a good, all-round view and feel of the form. Hand shears are the tool to use, but on larger trees, a long-armed hedge pruner can be useful if you need extra reach to get in towards the centre.

OPPOSITE: **Box spirals.**

39

Mini standards work well in containers, their short trunks combining with the height of the pot to raise the lollipop to a suitable height. The jury is out as to how well any plant grows in a pot, but topiary is definitely one of the better bets, as the regular clipping reduces demands on the roots for nutrients and water—think of clipping as acting like a growth retardant. Plants should be fed and watered well, and repotted every two or three years—Versailles-style planters with removable sides are the best long-term solution. Ultimately though, plants will always be happier planted in the ground than in pots.

A quick word now on epicormic growth: pruning of any sort inevitably results in a degree of epicormic growth—adventitious and slightly annoying shoots that emerge from the trunk. The harder the pruning, the more likely this is to occur, though some species are more prone to it than others. Normally it is not a problem, with the new growth being removed as and when necessary, but with standards it becomes more important to preserve the formal line of the bare trunk. If it becomes a problem, one alternative—particularly with yew standards which can get very bushy up the trunk, with rich new growth bursting out of the old, flaky bark—is to embrace the new growth and to clip it into a sleeve up the trunk, like pipe lagging or those funny, fluffy bantams' legs.

....

PAGE 40, TOP: *Robinia pseudoacacia* standards at Heale House, Wiltshire, England.
PAGE 40, BOTTOM: Regular *Ficus microcarpa* standards in California, U.S.A. Photo by David Davis.
PAGE 41: Yew standards. St Mary's church, Painswick, England.
OPPOSITE: Recently clipped box balls and a westernized variation on Japanese *niwaki* at Rosemary Alexander's Sandhill Farm House Garden, Hampshire, England.

TOPIARY MAINTENANCE

There is no room for indecision in the topiarist's vocabulary, nor sentimentality—a certain degree of dictatorship is called for, as is enthusiasm and above all an understanding of your role in the relationship. The one problem with topiary is that it keeps on growing—a common trait in most plants. It gets bigger, loses its shape and needs clipping, at least once a year, for the rest of its life. A lot of people seem to instinctively know how to clip. It comes naturally to them and they never need to think about it. Others find the whole thing slightly unsettling. They like topiary, they want topiary, and yet the physical action of clipping is a struggle. If I had to give one piece of advice regarding clipping, it would be to go for it. Clip hard, be brave and learn from your mistakes.

The trick is to clip as hard as you dare each year, not letting yourself be swayed by the luxurious new growth (none of that sentimentality), but cutting right back to within a fraction of the previous year. Inevitably, the shape will change over time, gradually getting larger, no matter how vigilant you have been, so every few years or so, have a good cut back, reshaping the plant if necessary. Spring or early summer is a generally a good time to do this, giving a full growing season for the plant to get back into shape. Box and most evergreens respond well to this heavy pruning, as does yew, but most conifers are not so obliging—a good reason not to use them in the first place.

With all clipping, hedges and topiary alike, clearing cut leaves and twigs from the plant is essential. Cut foliage is easy to miss, only becoming obvious weeks later when it turns brown. Yew can be the worst culprit, leaving little pockets of dead bits that stand out amongst the rich dark green. Try to clip from the top downwards, constantly shaking or knocking cut foliage off as you go, but do be careful that there are no nesting birds inside the plant before you shake.

The other trick to watch out for, again particularly with yew hedges and topiary, is growth that lies flat

against the sides of the plant. When using mechanical hedge cutters, or working quickly, there is a tendency to miss this growth, as it can slip under the blades. This is not a problem in the short-term, but over time these small shoots will turn woody and bulk up the outline of the shape. The following year, the temptation will be to prune over them, rather than through them, but this will eventually lead to swollen, varicose vein-like lumps that will ruin the shape of the project. Taking more care when pruning is the solution, but if a few slip through, cut them out with secateurs, even if it means revealing a gap or hole beneath. The gap will soon fill in, making this a far better long-term solution.

On the physical action of clipping, everyone has a different approach—slow, deliberate, fast or fluid. I tend to work quickly, often not actually cutting much in one snip, but clipping with a purpose and rhythm. Most shears are angled slightly—use the angle to your advantage on curves and diagonal planes. Find a balance between caution and confidence—work at a steady, determined pace but be prepared to stand back, assess and backtrack if need be.

How often to clip?

In the UK, yew is traditionally clipped only once a year, quite late in the summer, while box gets two clips, once in early summer and then a tidy up in early autumn, but that is a generalization: with larger scale topiary, you can get away with less clipping, but smaller or more detailed topiary demands more attention if you hope to keep it looking good. Whatever your approach—this is a highly personal thing, reflected in your garden as a whole—it pays to have tightly clipped outlines over the winter, when frosty mornings and low light can set off topiary beautifully, making it look its very best. I describe the difference between unclipped shapes and sharp, freshly clipped ones as the difference between a slightly out of focus image viewed through a camera lens and one that is fully focused. The former may look fine at first glance, but that extra tweak makes all the difference.

Tools

I must point out that I am biased here. I run a business selling Japanese pruning tools, amongst other things. Blatant self-promotion aside, a good pair of shears is absolutely essential. They come in various shapes and sizes, but the key points to look for when buying are good balance, simple design (as few moving or superfluous parts as possible) and high-quality steel. Once you start using them, it is crucial to keep them relatively clean (so the blades do not clog up with gunk) and sharp. I sharpen my shears throughout the day when I work, and the difference is remarkable. Sharp blades cut cleanly through leaves, while tired, blunt ones tear and rip, making a mess and clogging the blades.

Clogged blades can never be completely avoided, especially when box clipping, but by keeping a bucket of water with you when you clip, and dunking the blades in every so often, the resin will not get a chance to dry and stick to the blades. Some people prefer spraying with a mister—either way works, and if you are concerned by box blight, add a dash of bleach to the water to sterilize the blades between plants.

Japanese shears tend to have wooden handles and are longer than Western ones, providing better balance and a greater range of holding positions. I personally would avoid anything with plastic handles, as the join from handle to blade can be a weak point. I would also stay well clear of wavy-edged blades, which I find extremely difficult to sharpen. Generally speaking, it seems that, as with so much in life, extra features only distract from the important business at hand. Getting the best quality tools available, Japanese or otherwise, and looking

OPPOSITE, TOP: **Watch out for shoots on the sides of topiary and hedges, especially on yew.**
OPPOSITE, BOTTOM, LEFT: **Japanese shears with long wooden handles.**
OPPOSITE, BOTTOM, RIGHT: **Mechanical hedge cutters have their place in the topiary garden—here some electric ones are making short work of a double row of irregular box balls.**

after them well, is by far the most rewarding route to go down.

Mechanical hedge cutters have their place too, whether fuel-powered, electric or battery operated. Personally I rarely use them, preferring my trusty shears, but there is no denying they speed up the work and when handled well, can give a good finish. Electric models have the advantage of being much lighter, while battery operated ones are more portable. The fuel powered ones, while much heavier, are more powerful and are generally favoured by professionals. Some models offer 'topiary grade' teeth which give a finer cut and a tidier finish, and more recently battery-operated versions of these have also come on to the market. One solution to the pitfalls of working with hedge cutters is to use them just for the rough work and then go over the detailed bits with shears.

OPPOSITE: **Russian dolls in the mist at Marqueyssac.**

TWO
Cloud Pruning and Organic Topiary

A LOT OF PEOPLE THINK of topiary as being formal, geometric and slightly old-fashioned. I suppose it can be associated with a certain scale and grandeur that might not apply to everyone's garden, even though in reality topiary can fit into any setting, however modest. While this book focuses strongly on gardens that approach topiary in a fresh, individual style, it is worth backtracking to look at, in my opinion, the mother of all topiary gardens, Levens Hall in Cumbria, England.

Levens Hall has one of the most spectacular collections of yew and box topiary imaginable, in all shapes and sizes. It is packed with traditional topiary shapes such as multi-tiered wedding cakes, pyramids, spirals, top hats and mutated chess pieces, but look further and all is not as it should be: some forms have taken on a decidedly organic character, as though they were made of wax and exposed to the sun for too long. Definition is lost, in favour of natural, flowing lines. The landscape of Cumbria is called to mind: the dark, looming hills of the Lake District, one moment shrouded by heavy rain clouds, the next brilliantly illuminated as the clouds race on.

There are forms that could pass for a cubist rendition of a tree here (who knows, Picasso did like experimenting with his materials) that are not dissimilar to Japanese *niwaki*, the garden trees that are pruned and shaped to fit seamlessly into the landscapes of Japanese gardens. Speaking to Chris Crowder, the current head gardener at Levens Hall, who has worked there for 23 years, I was interested in knowing if there were any Japanese influences on any of the topiary in his garden, but it turned out that the topiary here was more the result of various generations of gardeners gradually asserting their own influences, along with time, the weather and the trees' own feelings coming into play. Heavy snowfalls, collapsed trees and various other natural problems over the years have affected the shapes of the topiary at Levens Hall as much as the gardeners themselves, with the response of the current team being to work with, rather than against, these setbacks.

When walking round the gardens, what struck me most at Levens Hall was the way that the individual yew trees blend together to create a surreal landscape, a wonderland of shapes. Some are strong and boldly defined, while others slip, quietly and slowly, into some otherworldly slumber, reverting back to the natural world from whence they came. My visit to this garden reminded me that the art of topiary is not the controlling of plants, but a collaboration with them, pruner and plant working together. No matter how sharp the shears, or keen the eye, the tree will always contribute its own presence to any pruning project, and inevitably, over time, it will prevail.

So, from my own point of view, having singled out what I find exciting about a garden such as Levens Hall—the wonky, gone native shapes rather than the formal stuff—it does not take long to appreciate that, in England at least, such examples of organic topiary are everywhere. Without straying far from my native county of Dorset, I began stumbling across them wherever I went. They often appeared in the form of hedges—

OPPOSITE: **Yew hedge at Beaminster, Dorset, England.**

49

examples such as these are usually known as cloud pruned hedges, although I have never entirely got on with this term, finding it to be too vague, as it describes not only big, old, billowing hedges but also Japanese garden trees too. A better description, I have decided, is organic topiary—the complete opposite to formal, classical topiary—which reflects the natural systems, landscapes and phenomena around us.

One of my favourites of all the big, bulbous, yew hedges is the one at Brampton Bryan in Herefordshire, England. It surrounds the church and grounds of the Harley Estate like a row of resting elephants, or perhaps decayed sand castles on the beach that have been almost washed away by the waves. They spill over the wall of the estate with all the yeasty energy of a home-baked loaf. A drive through the countryside around Brampton and further west into Wales offers glimpses into where the form of Brampton's hedges might come from. The Welsh term for the particular topography of the area, the lumps and bumps that make up the glorious landscape here, is *twmp* and the hedges at Brampton Bryan seem heavily in debt to them. They are defined by light, and the light in Wales comes flooding across the hills in glorious dashes, showing itself as a magic presence before being chased away by ominous, dark clouds.

Set in the chalky landscape of Wiltshire, England, the lovely village of Winterbourne Dauntsey has some fantastic old box hedges, particularly at one private home, The Grange. The gardens here were renovated by the current owner some 25 years ago, and one of the first jobs of the project was to reshape the overgrown hedges. Clipped once a year, they have settled into being fine examples of the art, in a very English setting. Vast, writhing, slightly intestinal worm-like forms line the drive, arching and twisting like The Very Hungry Caterpillar.

Interestingly, the same lane in Winterbourne Dauntsey has a fine example of a topiary peacock. The plume of the peacock merges with the thatched roof of the cottage in which garden it stands, reminding me of the well-known thatched cottages and box hedges of Chipping Campden in the Cotswolds, posing the question: does it get any more English than this?

Hedges such as those at Brampton Bryan and Winterbourne Dauntsey are still clearly rooted in their origins and function. They are still effectively hedges and their form, however unusual, fits roughly into the physical norm of what we expect a hedge to be. Venture into the depths of West Dorset however, to the pretty town of Beaminster, and the notion of what constitutes a hedge has been stretched to its limits. Once again, it is yew that is the culprit (although within the gardens there also lurk some fairly substantial box trees and one or two very impressive *Phillyrea latifolia*). From the outside, the boundaries of the property are fairly well kept, but the outline of the hedge owes more to the stunning coastline of West Dorset than to a town garden. The exaggerated outlines of Golden Cap, the highest point on the South Coast, not so far to the south of here, seem to have crept into play in these hedges, as anyone who has attempted its steep ascents and knee-jarring descents will testify.

The boundary restrictions on the outside of this yew hedge have had a predictable effect on the inside— such a vast hedge had to grow somewhere, and as it could not go out, it went in: great swollen globules of it have spilled out on to the lawns like melted ice caps or beached whales. Some plants are individually defined, while others flow seamlessly into larger shapes. Smooth, flowing lines are punctuated by looming, dolphin-like humps. Seen at different times of day, the yew takes on new characteristics. The rich green of the foliage in

....

PAGE 50: **Topiary in all shapes and sizes at Levens Hall, Cumbria, England.**
PAGE 51: **Cubist tree, Levens Hall, Cumbria, England.**
OPPOSITE, TOP: **The hedge at Brampton Bryan.**
OPPOSITE, BOTTOM, LEFT: **Organic topiary at Levens Hall, Cumbria, England.**
OPPOSITE, BOTTOM, RIGHT: **Box hedge in Winterbourne Dauntsey, Wiltshire, England.**

the sun turns a threatening black in the shade, while at dusk, the dark shapes are silhouetted in a still, foreboding manner.

Clipping this hedge is an autumn job, taking a good week for the gardener, using a collection of ladders, a portable scaffolding stage and a long-reach hedge trimmer. No hand shears here, due to the scale of the yew, but when watching the gardener at work, it is obvious that as much care and skill goes into using the hedge trimmer as it would on any smaller scale job with shears.

It is interesting to compare the organic yew topiary of Beaminster with the azalea *karikomi* of Japan. Much *karikomi* is on a fairly small scale, with individually clipped blobs often no more than 2 ft. (60 cm) high. At Shisendo-in, north east of Kyoto, however, huge banks of azaleas flank a path, effectively doing the job of a hedge. As at Beaminster, the influence of the landscape here seems instrumental—on a larger scale, this could be the tree-clad mountains of Japan that run down the spine of the country. Consciously or not, nature is at the root of all these hedges.

One last piece of organic topiary that deserves a mention and is also close to home in Dorset is perhaps the most remarkable of the lot. Tucked away behind the A35 road lives a remarkable yew tree, and this really is a tree, in size, shape and proportion. Whereas most of the organic topiary one comes across is in the guise of hedges or other forms of rounded topiary, this is a free-standing tree, at least 30 ft. (10 m) tall. Its story began back in the 1930s when the tree, growing close to the owner's house and becoming a liability, was cut back. It

was chopped at around 8 ft. (2.4 m), leaving a straight trunk that was expected to re-sprout, but rather than sending out new growth from the top, it sent out suckers from the base, one of which became dominant and started a second life for the tree. Twenty years ago, still being so close to the house, this new tree needed pruning too, so it was cut back to a framework of branches. That framework became the structure of the present tree, and since then it has been shaped and clipped every year. Even more amazing than the tree itself is the fact that the owner is in his 80s and spends most of August on the yearly clip, using a collection of ladders to get at all the branches and to climb into the canopy of the tree itself, from where he can reach the very highest central parts.

Over the years, this tree's branches have got denser and denser—they started off virtually bare, and gradually thickened up—until now the whole thing resembles a massive head of broccoli as much as anything else. The annual clip is done entirely with hand shears, but what is interesting to me is how similar this tree's creation was to that of Japanese *niwaki*. Cutting back evergreens and conifers to provide a new framework for them to grow to is known as *fukinaoshi* in Japan, a common nursery practice which literally translates as to re-do or start again. The new foliage that emerges from the cut branches is then trained and clipped into shape, giving the character of a mature tree in a more contained scale.

The tree in Dorset is unique among the yew topiary of England in that it is the only one that I know of that is pruned, in a perverse way, to resemble a tree—something that places it nearer the Japanese tradition of *niwaki* than the English tradition of organic topiary. The idea that one might deliberately prune a tree—and a large one at that—into a tree shape, rather than a geometric, topiarised form, might seem slightly absurd to some people, but it all makes perfect sense when the effect is actually seen in the flesh—by recreating a tree in this manner, both its character and that of the creator

PAGE 54: **Yew peacock topiary. Can it get any more English than this?**
PAGE 55, TOP: **Yew hedge, Beaminster, Dorset, England.**
PAGE 55, BOTTOM: **This organically shaped box hedge at Chipping Campden, Oxfordshire, England, complements the thatched roof.**
OPPOSITE, TOP: **The yearly clip, Beaminster, England.**
OPPOSITE, BOTTOM: **Evergreen azaleas at Shisendo-in, Kyoto, Japan.**

The *fukinaoshi* process practised in Japan results in a mature tree on a small scale.

are evident, an essence of tree as perceived by the artist. Similarly shaped trees are to be found in the Retiro Park in Madrid, where specimens of *Cupressus sempervirens* are pruned into large, brain-like topiary. At first sight, these trees seem at odds with their surroundings, out of context and slightly surreal, especially considering that they are Italian cypresses and have no right to be growing in this shape, but on further inspection, they sit comfortably within their formal environment and are a strong reminder of what is possible with a sharp pair of shears and a bit of cunning.

ELSEWHERE

Organic topiary and cloud pruning, when applied to hedges, seem to be thoroughly British habits, but they are not uniquely so. The large yew and box hedges of English country homes may be the original instigators, but the term 'cloud pruning' does not appear to have been commonly used until describing the likes of the designer Jacques Wirtz's work—in particular that in his own garden in Schoten, Belgium. Nowadays, thanks to

this garden, the name Wirtz is synonymous with cloud pruned hedges, but in fact he uses them only occasionally, preferring a more architectural kind of topiary and hedging to define his gardens.

Wirtz's garden at Schoten was never designed in the formal sense, as one might have expected. Instead, it was initially planted as a kind of in-house nursery, largely with box, to be used in future projects. The bones of the garden, the long, writhing hedges, were already there in the shape of overgrown box hedges planted along the axis of the garden. These hedges and an avenue of apple trees are all that remain of the garden that Wirtz inherited in 1969, originally the kitchen gardens of a local eighteenth century estate (he lives in the gardener's house). They provide a formal grid to the garden, adding maturity, a sense of time and proportion.

OPPOSITE, TOP: **The owner in action.**
OPPOSITE, BOTTOM, LEFT: **Organically shaped yew tree, Dorset, England.**
OPPOSITE, BOTTOM, RIGHT: *Cupressus sempervirens* **at the Retiro Park, Madrid, Spain.** Photo by Jacinta Lluch.

Within the grid of the box hedges lie rows of nursery stock, now well past their sell-by date. Over the years, as plants have been sold, the rows have lost some of their uniformity, so now there is a fascinating balance between the formal and the informal, the intentional and accidental. Box balls, blobs, cones, cubes and all shapes in between share space with unusual deciduous trees and other evergreens. In one area, a row of block-like rectangles, clipped into low slabs, offer a strong horizontal plane from behind which pops a collection of various balls and obelisks. Elsewhere, ranks of eggs and obelisks stand gathered in huddles, rather like Anthony Gormley's Terracotta Army figures, squeezed into their allotted space and slowly outgrowing it.

I visited in late October, on a mild autumn day. All the box had been clipped—there is so much of it at Wirtz's garden that they do not have the luxury of perfect timing, so some had scorched a bit from bright sun—and there was a pleasant end of year, slightly laid-back feel to the garden. Box clippings lay around some of the more recently clipped shapes, and the bare earth of the nursery beds made no pretenses towards being anything grander than it was.

What I came away with from my visit was the sense of the visual excitement to be had from the juxtaposition of shapes—the flat planes and spheres, the mishmash of overlapping and interlocking outlines, other strong shapes highlighted by foliage behind. The cloud pruned hedges themselves were of course fantastic, for their quality, scale and role within the garden. Ironically, one would expect to have formally clipped hedges defining the layout in a garden like this, and in its previous incarnation that was the case, before Wirtz got his hands on it. The hedges he inherited were overgrown, but had once been clipped into low, formal edging. Rather than restoring them to their original form, Wirtz took to the shears and followed the overgrown contours suggested by the plants themselves, looking to natural forms for his inspiration. Originally, he did all the clipping himself over the summer and later his sons Martin and Peter, who now work together in the family design practice, helped out.

Heading to Asia now, big organic hedges like this are less common here than in Europe. The Japanese tend to prune more intentionally, with more definition. Hedges as we know them are relatively scarce, replaced instead by individual trees. Off the mainland of Korea, however, at the Botania gardens on Oedo island, there are some extraordinary examples of topiary and some fantastic hedges. A privately owned island, the garden was started in 1976 after initial farming exploits there failed. I have not had the opportunity to visit, but from what I have seen, this appears to be a remarkable pleasure garden, in a spectacular setting in the South Korean sea. On their website, the name Oedo is turned neatly into the acronym for Oriental Exotic Dream Oasis. Within the garden, there is the Stairway to Heaven, the Paradise Lounge and the Venus garden, giving one a good idea of what is on offer.

Built into the slopes of the island, the garden is defined by the constant use of *Juniperus chinensis* 'Kaizuka' that flow through it. Billowing cloud hedges break the slope up into terraces, flowing along the contours of the hillside. To my eye, they seem decidedly Eastern: I can see dragons—angry ones—etched into the hedges, and leaving aside my complete ignorance of the Korean script (*hangul*) I also fancy that I can read cryptic messages carved into the reliefs.

The hedges give way to covered walkways, made up of double rows of juniper with clear trunks. Their tops have merged together and are clipped into flat, globular slabs, like a thick, viscous liquid that has set solid—toffee perhaps. Seen from above, they take on the form of layers of clouds that are floating down the slope in drifts, waiting for the heat of the day to clear them. Acting as pergolas, they are an interesting variation on the organic, cloud pruned theme—raised cloud pruned hedges, if such a

....

OPPOSITE: **Jacques Wirtz's cloud pruned hedges at Schoten.**

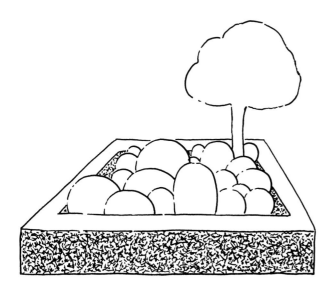

Ideas for hedges, inspired by Jacques Wirtz

term exists. Whenever I see rows of clipped plants of any sort growing on hillsides like this, my mind wanders to tea plantations. There is something immensely satisfying about the tiered repetition of tea plantations, the way they follow the contours of the slopes they are grown on, that exciting balance of organic and man-made.

Creating an organic, cloud pruned hedge

Before looking at the practicalities of pruning and forming cloud pruned hedges and organic topiary, it is worth thinking about what draws us to them in the first place. Visually, they appear soft and comforting, yet also bold and sculptural. Despite being so unusual, they perform as all good hedges should, creating a boundary, screen, and backdrop to the garden. They look good and they serve a purpose. More than that though, I think the

....

PAGE 62, TOP: **Cubes, eggs, and balls share nursery beds at Schoten, Belgium.**
PAGE 62, BOTTOM: **Double rows of flat-topped junipers line the hillside at Oedo-Botania. Photo by J.S. Gim.**
PAGE 63: **Hedges at Oedo-Botania, Oedo Island, South Korea.** Photo by J. S. Gim.

reason that we find them so fascinating and that they work so well in the garden, in particular English gardens, is because they are imbued with something of the natural landscape—in them we see the woods, the fields and especially the gentle, rolling hills that is the English countryside. Subconsciously, we are drawn to these forms, perhaps even without realizing it, because they are a deeply rooted part of our lives. The shapes that these old hedges assume are always organic, comforting ones: vegetables like mushrooms, broccoli and root ginger; large, friendly mammals such as elephants and dolphins; freshly baked bread; and even squidgy body parts.

Cloud pruning an existing hedge

Creating a billowing, cloud pruned hedge out of an existing hedge is one of the most exciting projects available to the creative pruner, as well as being relatively simple and surprisingly quick. Yew (usually *Taxus baccata*) is the standard for this sort of project, and occasionally box (usually *Buxus sempervirens*) is used on a smaller scale, but when following this method the beauty is that you get what you are given. Making the best of it is what defines and highlights the character

Got this . . .   . . . want this

of the hedge. Any hedge that is healthy is a potential target—even the dreaded Leyland cypress (×*Cupressocyparis leylandii*), although that will keep you busy over the summer months, and of course can not be cut back too hard.

As with topiary in general, evergreens are the obvious choice, but in fact deciduous hedge species also have their place. Beech (species of *Fagus*) will keep its brown leaves through the winter, and even fully deciduous trees can be attractive, creating a ghost-like tension in the winter and often carrying berries or spring blossoms before coming back into leaf. Mixed hedges will also work and in some cases help in the decision making process that follows.

The big question is though, how to turn something so ordered and formal into something so spontaneous and organic? Well, the more irregularities, the better. It can help to leave the hedge unpruned for a year or two before starting, to encourage natural strengths and weaknesses to surface—the more vigorous plants within the hedge will expand, while others might fall behind and weaker plants might actually die out. Mixed hedges will naturally have different growth rates, which adds to the irregularity. A year or two of neglect will raise a few possibilities and almost suggest a form by itself.

Out of context from the rest of the garden, it would be fine to leave the design entirely up to nature, but within the garden, think about how the hedge will fit. Will it be functioning as a screen and should therefore be of a certain height, at least in places? Will it be echoing shapes beyond, perhaps drawing in contours and silhouettes of the surrounding landscape, rather like the Japanese sense of *shakkei* (borrowed scenery)? Will the hedge be a smooth, flowing affair or a huge, carbunculous monster? With these considerations in mind, it is a good idea to make a couple of quick sketches as a starting point, of what you have got to start with and what you intend—nothing fancy, just simple strong lines, like the hedge itself.

With a collection of tools—shears, secateurs and even mechanical hedge trimmers, set to. Rough out basic forms, following the flow of the plants. Do not be afraid to cut right back into the hedge (you ought to know by now which plants will respond well to being cut back hard and which ones die back), even removing individual plants completely if necessary, to open up the solid volume.

Think not only about height and silhouette, but also depth—will the hedge spill out onto the lawn (like the pastry on a good pie), or should it be more contained? Space permitting, encourage as much variation as possible (it can always be ironed out later if it seems too intentional). Avoid too much repetition, aiming for a natural irregularity, which is, of course, much harder than nice ordered formality. This is where your personal character comes into play—some people are inevitably more cautious, others more confident (not to be confused with recklessness, mind). Enjoy the process and take your time—come back to it over the year, digging deeper than you dared previously. The hedge will almost certainly look like a complete mess by the time you have finished with it, but that is okay, it will soon grow back and fill in any evidence of excess enthusiasm.

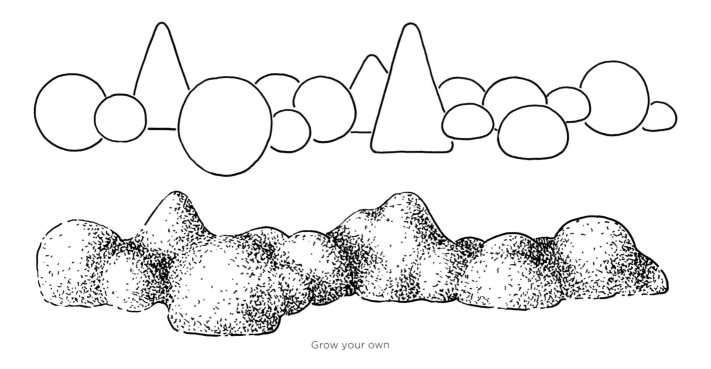

Grow your own

Making a cloud pruned hedge from scratch

Creating a hedge from scratch could be compared with the trick of distressing new furniture to give it character and make it look old, or intentionally ripping your jeans. It works, but never quite as satisfyingly as doing it the slow way, letting time add character. As with so much in the garden, time is the master.

So, where to begin? If you have less time than money, there is a short cut. Thoughtful nurseries have started growing ready-made cloud hedges, planted in rows to be numbered, root balled and replanted in formation. This is the quickest solution, and its off-the-shelf appearance is not to be sniffed at, for the techniques used to get it this far are exactly the same as you would use when doing it yourself. Scale is an issue here though, as inevitably the size of the hedge is limited by what is available for sale. One nursery I visited in Belgium, Solitair, had an enormous piece of box for sale, the size and shape of a resting elephant, but this was an exception, and more often the material available is much smaller. Tom Stuart-Smith used this approach in his 2010 Royal Horticultural Society (RHS) Chelsea garden, arranging established box balls into a shape to give the impression of a far older, more mature hedge, although interestingly he chose not to clip them for the show, preferring a softer look that was more in keeping with the rest of the planting. Once planted in situ, it would only take another year or two for the lines of the box to become more fluid, were some of the shapes allowed to flow into each other.

A more hands-on, halfway compromise is to buy a collection of topiary balls of varying sizes, as well as a few cones to add vertical presence and to plant them in a row, creating the bones of a hedge. Look for irregular arrangements and think about how the hedge will look within the context of the garden. Allow a degree of depth to the hedge, and introduce varying height with

PAGES 66-67: **This hedge, recently renovated by topiary specialist Nicky Fraser, stands out but also sits perfectly within the surrounding countryside.** Photo by Danny Beath.
OPPOSITE: **Tom Stuart-Smith's 2010 RHS Chelsea Flower Show garden.**
PAGE 70-71: **Section of ready-made cloud pruned hedge at the Solitair nursery, Belgium.** Photo by NV Solitair.

the cones. An important question is how close to plant: no doubt you intend the hedge to fill out from the original size of the balls and cones, so you will want to leave some space between each plant, but knowing how much depends on your expectations.

Finally, the long-term, low budget and perhaps most satisfying solution, is to first plant young hedging plants, exactly as if you were planting a formal hedge. Small, bushy plants, planted 8–12 in. (20–30 cm) apart for box or 18–24 in. (45–60 cm) apart for yew, perhaps in a double, alternate row to add depth. This way, the hedge develops at its own pace, keeping it nice and dense the whole way through. For the first few years, pinch out the growth with secateurs or shears to help it consolidate and fill out. Right from the start, some plants will be more vigorous than others, but these differences should be exploited. If plants die out, there is no need to replace them, as the empty space will soon be filled from either side.

All that holds you back from now on is your imagination. As you and the hedge find a natural equilibrium, your creative role will give way to one of maintenance. Keeping any topiary in shape is much the same as a regular hedge, but something many people have trouble understanding is how to keep it the same size—how to stop it from getting too big. The answer, unsurprisingly, is pruning. Luckily, organic topiary is more forgiving than its more straight-laced siblings—there are no straight lines or tricky corners. Although there will come a point where the hedge is definitely finished, it can continue to grow and evolve with yearly clips, with more detail able to be added to large, featureless shapes, or overworked areas being filled in and simplified—it is all down to you.

THREE

Hedges

HEDGES—LIKE THEM OR NOT, they play a crucial role in most gardens. However, rather than existing solely as the perimeter, backdrop, windbreak or screen to a garden, it is when the humble hedge is made into something more creative that it becomes a feature in its own right, on an equal footing with topiary, borders or lawns. If you will excuse the pun, it is time to think outside the box.

To start with, let's look at what makes a good hedge. Deciduous or evergreen is the first question. In Europe and much of North America, deciduous hedges in the garden tend to be most commonly planted with beech (species of *Fagus*) or hornbeam (species of *Carpinus*), both of which hang onto their leaves during winter, or dense, thorny species such as *Crataegus* or various *Prunus*. The notion that deciduous hedges are less dense in winter is only partly true. *Crataegus* and others tend to get so dense after a while that they become an almost solid mass, even in the depths of winter, while the brown leaves of beech and hornbeam allow for the character of a semi-permeable hedge, which filters through valuable light on gloomy afternoons.

Evergreen hedges come in all shapes and sizes, depending on location (hardiness), trends (thankfully, it looks like we are coming to the end of the Leyland cypress trend at last) and purpose (speed of growth, eventual size, etc.) Yew and box are the heroes of hedges, ×*Cupressocyparis leylandii* the villain, but nearly all evergreens also have something to offer.

....

OPPOSITE: **Crenellated hornbeam hedges at Jacques Wirtz's garden, Schoten, Belgium.**

The key to a good hedge is its batter—the angle of its sides. To allow enough light to the lower half of the hedge, it should be wider at the base than at the top. It is an exaggeration to say that without the right batter the hedge is doomed, but it will certainly struggle to remain healthy and dense from top to bottom. One rarely notices good batter, but top-heavy hedges with bad batter that balance precariously like upturned chunks of cheese and are inevitably bald at the bottom, stand out like a sore thumb.

Next up is the formative pruning of young hedges, to ensure that they are dense and bushy at the base to start with. The traditional approach is to cut back new or recently planted hedging plants, to prepare good foundations. Thinner, more straggly plants such as species of *Crataegus*, *Prunus*, *Buxus* and even *Lonicera nitida* all need pruning right from the start to encourage a good foundation. This means cutting back quite hard into the plant after planting, repeating this the next year. Other species, beech and hornbeam for example, should be cut back by up to one-third of the leader and side branches. Bushy conifers like yew, for example, need very little formative pruning.

In much of northern Europe, the practice is to plant much taller, thinner nursery stock than is common in Britain and to plant them far closer together. An example of this can be seen at Jacques Wirtz's garden in Belgium, where tall, narrow hornbeam hedges create an elegant screen at the front of the house. I always enjoy coming across small differences like this between different cultures—books and education normally tend to toe the line, but something as common as hedging

Good batter ... bad batter

OPPOSITE: A mixed hedge of *Lonicera nitida* (green and variegated), *Prunus cerasifera* and box.
ABOVE: Hornbeam hedges at Jacques Wirtz's garden in Schoten, Belgium.

often becomes ingrained in our minds without much thought: plant small, cut back to make bushy. Yet across the Channel, in places closer to London than my own home, we see almost exactly the opposite, reminding me that there is still plenty of room left for the inquisitive gardener. In something as personal as one's own garden, so many opportunities arise from keeping an open mind. I wonder what they do in Norway?

THE HEDGE AS ARCHITECTURE

So, rather than looking at how to grow a good hedge, which when it comes down to it, most people figure out for themselves without too much trouble, let's look at how to make hedges more interesting—by using them as architecture and promoting them to a more assertive role in the garden. There are architectural features that are directly related to their stone and brick namesakes—buttresses, crenellations, windows, arches, niches, whole rooms even, but there are also pleached hedges, hedges on stilts, double and triple hedges, even mazes. Then there is design, and the use of the hedge not as a hedge at all, but as sculpture. And size. Very big, or wide hedges have a character all of their own. So whether your hedge is one of centuries-old yew, common privet, or even gloomy conifers, all sorts of things are possible.

Buttresses

When it comes to cathedrals, buttresses come in various shapes and sizes (remember flying buttresses?), but in the garden they are used not for structural reasons, but for visual impact. One normally comes across them in formal topiary gardens, appearing to prop up yew hedges. By breaking up the hedge, they make a series of bays that offer up all sorts of opportunities: if the hedge is at the back of a lawn, then benches and sculptures can fit snugly in the bays, framed by a buttress on either side. If it is at the back of a border, then the border can be planted up in themes; if in a kitchen garden, then vegetables can be planted in rotated beds.

They also make great places for games, and of course provide perfect firing positions and cover from imaginary enemy onslaughts. If, as has happened at Shakespeare's New Place Museum in Stratford upon Avon, one neglects one's buttresses and they turn from the imposing architectural things they were intended to be into great, swollen carbuncles, then they still serve similar purposes, with the added charm of a tumbledown country cottage, as if made of slowly decomposing hay bales rather than well-clipped yew.

Battlements and crenellations

I imagine that most crenellated hedges are instigated by men, old men probably, for they are the logical progression from the sandcastles, camps and dens of childhood, for the young boy stuck inside the grown man. As with hedges in general, the character of the maker inevitably manifests itself in the results, so some crenellated hedges are tight and exact, while others are rather more shambolic, as if they have endured months of siege and heavy cannon fire.

The principles of crenellation construction are very simple. Once embarked on, it only takes a couple of years to turn some shaggy lumps at the top of the hedge into clearly defined fortifications. Ideally, the trunks of individual plants within the hedge should correspond with the merlons (the high bits) not the crenels (the low bits) as the growth of the trunks will be more vigorous—work with the hedge, not against it.

When it comes to clipping, unless you want your battlements to look like the Alamo, you need a bit of discipline to keep the tops of the merlons in line, the bottoms of the crenels flat, and the sides straight. Opting for the higgledy piggledy approach gives you more leeway for error, and the results can be just as effective.

....

OPPOSITE, TOP: **Zounds! Misshapen buttresses at New Place, Stratford, England.**
OPPOSITE, BOTTOM: **Crenellated hedges at Levens Hall, Cumbria, England.**

Windows

Windows in hedges are great—something as simple as a hole can add humour, surprise, depth, symbolism and even poetry to a garden. Just as windows in walls let in light and frame views, so do hedge windows, but somehow, because it is not the sort of thing one normally sees in the garden, it injects an element of surprise too—and who can resist poking their head through a good hole in a hedge?

The best windows are not necessarily planned, but often materialize out of a patch of poorly growing hedge, suggesting themselves first as holes. They only become windows when properly framed, which is the tricky bit to do well, especially in wider hedges, where light has trouble reaching in. The basic principle is to cut part of the hedge's foliage away with secateurs to reveal a rough window shape, taking care not to cut too much from the top of the hole, as the hedge will only regrow reluctantly from above. If need be, train down a thin branch to form the top frame. Start using shears or clippers to form dense frames, then clip as frequently as the rest of the hedge. Great fun could be had forming muntins from horizontal and vertical branches—and what is to stop them being glazed as well?

Arches

Nothing is more architectural in the garden than the arch. Used in the garden it takes the form of a gateway, an opening within a hedge. Extended into aqueducts, arches in the garden seem particularly popular in Germany—Schwetzingen Palace, for example, has a fine lime, or linden, aqueduct, echoing the real brick one that runs through the grounds. Essentially, this is a hedge with doors cut into it. It is flat along the top and each column is formed from one lime tree that is clipped close to the trunk for the vertical ascent, and allowed to connect on each side with the next tree. These arches seem as contrived as anything in the garden, even more so than much topiary, yet they fit in perfectly here,

thanks to their architectural reference, their scale, and in the case of Schwetzingen Palace, their quality.

In Costa Rica, meanwhile, are the extraordinary arches at the church of San Rafael in Zarcero. Maintained, as it has been since its creation in 1964, by Evangelisto Blanco Brenes, this kind of garden is only possible with a single, no doubt wildly eccentric, creator at the helm. Fantastic avenues and double avenues of arches line the paths to the church. Not formal, regular arches such as you would see in Europe, but a writhing array of stalagmites that could only have materialized on the same continent as the magical realism of Gabriel Garcia Marquez.

To recreate the wonderful shapes at Zarcero is surprisingly easy. They are formed out of two plants, planted as if part of an avenue (in fact, in this case I suspect that they did start life as a regular avenue). At the appropriate height, simply train the leaders in towards each other, bending down with wire or string and tie in with a cane. New growth from the trained beams is then clipped into shape, much like any topiary or hedge. Similar effects are seen all over the world in different guises: rose arches in cottage gardens spring to mind, as does yew in English churchyards. Indeed, it is interesting to compare the churchyard at Zarcero with the one at St Mary's Church Painswick in Gloucestershire, England. Most churchyards in the UK have a yew tree or two in their grounds, either free-growing or clipped, but St Mary's is no ordinary churchyard—there are hundreds of them here, pruned into individual standards and arches. Their form is less extraordinary than their Latin counterparts, more Laurie Lee than

....

OPPOSITE, TOP: **At what point does an arch become a tunnel? Miserden Church, Gloucestershire, England.**
OPPOSITE, BOTTOM, LEFT: **Lime arches at Schwetzingen Palace, Germany.** Photo by Michael Bell.
OPPOSITE, BOTTOM, RIGHT: **Zarcero, Costa Rica.** Photo by Kent Smith.

Garcia Marquez perhaps, but equally evocative of their environment.

In the case of San Rafael, the hedges there are a *Cupressus* species, most probably *Cupressus lusitanica*. While species of *Cupressus* respond well to regular light clipping in general, ultimately they are not ideal for topiary projects because, like many other conifer species, they resent being cut too hard. Clipping the new growth is fine, but cut back into the woody growth and they start to object, hence some of the arches at San Rafael having bald patches, particularly near the bottom of each plant, where the branching is older.

The Japanese have their own take on the arch, as they do with most things. Outside their homes it is common to train a side branch of a tree over the gateway, framing the approach. This can also be over the driveway, and often the branch extends further still, continuing beyond the gateway around the perimeter of the garden. The Japanese black pine (*Pinus thunbergii*) and the yew-like *Podocarpus macrophyllus* are popular material for this treatment, known as *monkaburi* in Japanese. Despite the unusual look, it really is only an extension of the standard training and pruning that they use for their *niwaki* (garden trees), and is also remarkably similar to fruit training techniques.

There comes a point with an arch where, if it gets too deep, it ceases being an arch and becomes a tunnel. Quite where that point lies is a good question, but it is obvious enough when it happens. Tunnels of solid hedge, especially those of evergreens and conifers, are difficult to grow because of the lack of light within the tunnel, but deciduous trees do much better when trained and pruned into shape. The same can be said for houses, igloos, and yurt-shaped domes, where hornbeam or beech are the material of choice (or ash in the case of the artist David Nash's dome).

Mazes

Unless one is seriously into topology, the scale of real mazes is beyond the reach of the average garden. Their attraction lies in the fun they bring, and the visual effect they create, especially when seen from above. The sculptural interplay of horizontal and vertical planes, whether flat-topped and formal or rounded and organic, brings a new dimension into the garden, especially in the right light—usually early morning or late afternoon, when the sun is low. From a sculptural point of view mazes are pretty similar to complicated parterres, although of course their function, and height, are rather different.

The azalea maze at the Getty Museum in Los Angeles, designed by artist Robert Irwin, is a great example of form over function and visually is one of the more interesting cases I have come across. Described as a floating maze, it is planted within a shallow pool and gives the impression of being inflated, like an elaborate lilo, or inflatable mattress. Surrounded by water, it cannot actually be walked through, so whether it qualifies as a maze at all is open to discussion.

Planted with evergreen kurume azaleas (*Rhododendron* species), it has more than a hint of Japanese influence to it—in fact, there is a strong Japanese influence to much of the pruning in California, where many Japanese have lived since the early twentieth century. The low, rounded forms are suggestive of Japanese *karikomi* pruning and tea plantations. Being azaleas they flower (mostly pink, with some white) in late spring. Cleverly, the dead ends are blocked with pillows of azalea, adding more tension and energy to the design than had they been solid masses joined to the sidewalls.

This maze is striking partly because of its unusual form (the low, sausage shapes) and being set in water, but also, crucially, because of the angle the public view it from—it was designed as part of the garden as a whole and all around it are raised banks so one always looks

....

PAGE 80: **St Mary's Church, Gloucestershire, England.**
PAGE 81: ***Monkaburi*, Japan.**
OPPOSITE, TOP: **The azalea maze at the Getty Museum, California, U.S.A.** Photo by Didier Morlot.
OPPOSITE, BOTTOM: **Azalea maze detail, Getty Museum, California. U.S.A.** Photo by Scott Woodruff.

down on it from above rather than at it, along the same horizontal plane. It is quite definitely designed to be looked at rather than explored, as an artwork rather than a maze, which might take the fun out of it, but this is what creates its marvellous sculptural presence.

Doubles and trebles

Hedges can also add a sculptural element to gardens through repetition. Double or triple hedges, either with varying heights or terraced down a slope, provide a strong interplay of horizontals and outlines, offering some of the visual excitement of the maze but on a less imposing scale. A simple laurel hedge (*Prunus laurocerasus*) I pass most days has three layers to it, sloping down to the road on what would ordinarily be a plain grass bank. The space between the hedges not only creates a sense of depth, but also provides useful access for clipping. It adds a feel of the exotic to a pretty dreary stretch of the road approaching Yeovil—the laurel itself could not be more suburban, but to me the stepped effect evokes tea plantations high in the hills, somewhere in the Far East.

The same effect is used in the Raikyu-ji temple in Okayama, Japan, where the clipped azalea *karikomi*, modelled on wave patterns, flows along the slope at the back of the garden. In sunlight, the fissures in the hedges are cast into deep shade, providing a strong contrast with the bright green leaves of the surface. The patterns of light and dark and the sheer, vertical cliff faces that are cut into the sloping bank create a much more abstract feel than the *karikomi* gardens at places such as Shisendo-in, as this appears to be much more like a three-dimensional, computer generated landscape rather than plant life. Again, this artificial landscape

....

OPPOSITE, TOP: **A bank of laurel made into an interesting triple hedge, Yeovil, Somerset, England.**
OPPOSITE, BOTTOM, LEFT: **Tea plantation in India.** Photo by David Davis.
OPPOSITE, BOTTOM, RIGHT: **Azalea *karikomi* at Raikyu-ji, Okayama, Japan.** Photo Robert Ketchell.

seems related to tea plantations, at the point where horticulture meets agriculture.

PLEACHED HEDGES AND RAISED HEDGES

There are few more sophisticated things possible in a garden than a pleached hedge. They bring a sense of architecture and formality to the garden, of structure and style. Even more than formal yew hedges, they imply a sense of grandeur. Look to the chateaux of France, the modernism of northern Europe and the stately homes of Britain for proof. With their straight trunks of hornbeam or lime and solid blocks of foliage on top, dividing and delineating, screening and revealing, they are a crucial tool in any formal garden.

First of all, let's get the terminology straight. The word pleach comes from the Latin *plectere*, to plait, which refers to the weaving together of branches. Interestingly, the term can also be applied to the rural art of hedge laying, where trees within old hedgerows are cut at the base, but not completely severed, and laid flat (or at an angle) to create foundations for new growth. From a practical point of view however, pleaching involves the training of side branches or trunks, but that is only half the story. The term is used to describe all sorts of variations on the theme and is interchangeable with 'raised' or 'stilted' hedge—the common factor in pleached hedges being bare trunks at the bottom.

Personally, I see room for more definition within the genre, both technically and aesthetically. I recognize four different models (much like early Volkswagens, funnily enough): type one is the pleached hedge whose top half, once trained into place, is clipped much like a normal hedge, creating a solid slab of foliage, with flat top, bottom and straight sides. The inner workings—the formative training—soon become secondary to the external solidity of the hedge.

Type two hedges, rather than being clipped, are pruned back each year to their skeletal framework, more like a two-dimensional pollard (a tree that is regularly

pruned back to its simplest trunk and branch structure) than a hedge. They tend to be less formal than their clipped counterparts, as they are not solid. They provide very little screening value over the winter, but have much more character, as over time the trained branches fuse together and develop swollen bolls, or lumps, where they are cut back to annually, creating stark, petrified silhouettes. Limes are the default choice here, as they respond so well to hard pruning. For the record, although type one seems to be the standard to which most people refer when talking about pleached hedges, type two is my favourite—they seem to be more involving, more personal than the clipped version. To confuse things though, occasionally one comes across a type one and a half, when a type two hedge is given a quick going over in mid summer to keep it in check, before being cut back properly in the winter.

Type three eschews training completely, so theoretically is not pleached at all, just stilted. Here trees are grown in a row, either as young plants or as more mature standards, with straight trunks that are raised to the desired height. The crowns are then allowed to grow away, and are clipped to the outline of the hedge. Externally, the results look similar to type one, especially over the summer, but internally the structure is less defined. They are the easiest of the four styles to grow, and the ideal cheat's solution: nurseries even supply square standards that can create an instant hedge on legs, for those with more cash than time.

Type one and type two are usually deciduous—hornbeam or lime—but type three, for cheats, can be almost anything. Evergreens such as *Quercus ilex* are ideal, as is yew, but there is no reason why virtually any large shrub or tree that makes a good hedge cannot be turned into a raised hedge. *Phillyrea latifolia* springs to mind, as it always does, in a default kind of way when I think about pruning projects, as does *Elaeagnus* ×*ebbingei*. I once experimented with a *Myrtus apiculata* raised hedge and that looked promising, especially with its velvet orange

bark and flowers. Ask yourself two questions: does it prune well, and can I stand looking at its bare trunk.

The fourth and final approach, for real desperados, is to raise an established hedge, much like raising individual trees, by cutting off all the lower branches up to a certain point. Inevitably, the trunks of the hedge will be irregular and much closer together than is normal, but for a sculptural look that is not necessarily a bad thing. Rabbits and livestock achieve something similar by grazing at the lower branches of rural hedges and revealing the character of the trunks. It is quick, easy, and surprisingly effective.

Focusing on type two, my favourite, I like to think of them as elongated pollards (those big knobbly things in France). They have the greatest presence in the winter when reduced to their skeletal form, with their leafless branches like bony arms, their swollen elbows and knuckles silhouetted by the low winter light. Each year's growth is pruned off during the winter, to regrow over the following summer, over time creating the lumpy bolls that are associated with pollarding.

It is these bolls that give the hedge character, but where pleaching differs from pollarding is the process of training and fusing the branches effectively into one very long tree. Planted as young trees, side branches are trained horizontally, usually along wires or frames, and are eventually allowed to grow into the space of the neighboring tree. When they touch, the branches slowly go through a process called inosculation, basically a natural form of grafting: movement between

OPPOSITE, TOP, LEFT: **Type one pleached hedge at Arley Hall, Cheshire, England. Around 150 years old, this is clipped once each year in September, but throughout the summer epicormic growth is grubbed off the trunks.** Photo by Maria Hiles.
OPPOSITE, TOP, RIGHT: **Type two: the bolls of an old, pleached lime hedge.**
OPPOSITE, BOTTOM: **Enormous cubed hornbeams for sale at the Solitair nursery in Belgium. Planted closer together, they would make a perfect type three hedge.** Photo by NV Solitair.

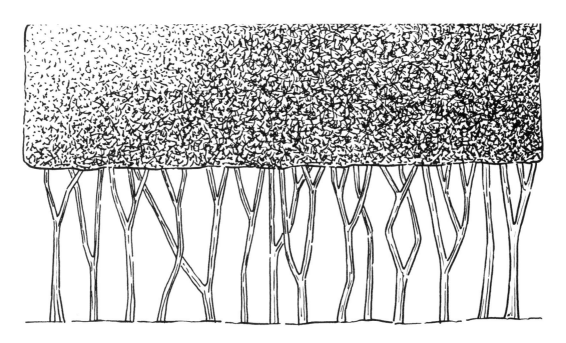

Type four: the look of a raised, established hedge

the two branches causes friction, which rubs away the outer layer of bark between them, revealing the cambium layer. The cambium layer is where all the action goes on, as when held together at this point, the two branches eventually fuse together. A similar thing can happen in the wild, when branches, often in the same tree, are forced together and join over time.

The lime is the pruning pleacher's tree of choice (as opposed to the clipping pleacher, who favours the hornbeam): *Tilia ×euchlora, T. cordata* and *T. platyphyllos* and most other *Tilia* species all respond well to heavy pruning. Once again, nurseries now conveniently sell starter kits for pleached hedges, where all the tricky work and decisions have been taken care of—they provide straight, uniform trunks with a bamboo system into which the horizontal levels of branching are trained. The only real problem of using these ready-mades is, by their very nature, they are a one-size-fits-all solution, grown as uniformly as possible. Tier spacing is prescribed, and if an instant effect is needed, so is the width of individual trees, although there is no reason why they should not be planted further apart and allowed to grow in over time, but the whole point of the ready-made is that there is no waiting, and they should thus be planted in a solid, continuous row.

As always, if time and imagination are two assets you are endowed with, going it alone is the best answer. You can decide the logistics of spacing, tier heights, number of tiers, etc., in relation to your own garden. Nursery pleaches tend to come in a standard square format, with three to four tiers of branching as close as 12 in. (30 cm) apart from each other—fine for a short run of screening, but to my mind too condensed for anything more ambitious.

The process of pleaching is straightforward, and quite similar to fruit tree training techniques such as the espalier. Decide on spacing—8 ft. (2.4 m) is about

right for a 10–12 ft. (3–3.6 m) hedge, but the taller the hedge, the wider the spacing can be. Laying good foundations from the outset is essential, as all decisions here are final. If the hedge is to have a double row, forming an avenue, it is even more important that the trees are perfectly spaced, and directly opposite each other.

Maintenance pruning is a winter job, removing all new growth, right back down to the old wood. Some pleachers choose to do this in the autumn, sometimes even before the leaf drop to catch the leaves before they fall. Others wait until early spring, enjoying the shaggy, over-wintered look and colour of the new growth—if I can get around to it, I like to prune in the autumn because I feel the stark, monochrome silhouettes of winter are what pleaching (and pollarding) is all about. Throughout the summer, feel free to remove any epicormic growth around the trunk if it bothers you—it is no problem to just prune or grub it off as and when.

The framework structure can stay up indefinitely, although after a while the individual bamboo canes become unnecessary. In the long-term, the weight of the side branches can start to weigh them down, so keeping the wires up can be useful, although sagging branches are one of the characteristics of old pleached hedges and having dead straight branches is not something to get obsessed by.

Both raised and pleached hedges tend to be associated with traditional large scale gardens, but on the Continent, especially in Belgium and Holland, they are a common feature in many smaller suburban gardens, More recently, they have become popular with smart designers in urban gardens, where the screening function of the hedge is a requirement, but something a little extra is needed visually. These gardens use the ready-made nursery trees for instant impact, but it is the big, old hedges in large, established gardens that are where the best examples lie.

Whatever scale one uses them on, both pleached and raised hedges have certain practical advantages over full hedges: more light reaches the ground, giv-

OPPOSITE: **Type three: an unusual raised *Phillyrea* hedge being turned into a row of bells.**

HOW TO MAKE A PLEACHED HEDGE

1. Dig holes and place stout end-posts (preferably guyed or braced) every 16 ft. (4.8 m) along the line where you would like your hedge to be (or between every other tree if the plants are already established). Tension wire between your end-posts for the tiers, starting at 6 ft. (1.8 m) from the ground. For a 12 ft. (3.6 m) tall hedge, create four tiers, spacing the wires evenly up to 11 ft. 6 in. (3.5 m). Position a 12 ft. (3.6 m) bamboo cane in the ground 4 ft. (1.2 m) from each end-post, then tie it into the wire, marking the intended place of the first tree. Repeat at exactly 8 ft. (2.4 m) intervals. Plant and tie your young trees into the canes, taking care to keep them exactly in line.

2. When the trees become tall enough, direct their side branches to grow along the wires, thus keeping the tree tied to the cane and the wires as it grows. Use rubber ties that stretch and/or string made of natural fibres (though this may need replacing after a year or so) to train the tree to its cane and wires. The branches may not be perfectly placed for tying down initially, so you may need to train them down slightly further or encourage them to grow up to the next level, but these discrepancies will lessen as the hedge takes shape. As the tied down side branches grow, tie down the new tips over winter and continue to train the leader to its vertical cane.

3. When the leader reaches the top tier, pinch it out to encourage side shoots. Train the side shoots across the top wire, and remove all subsequent top growth.

4. As the side branches begin to meet, tie them together to help with the inosculation grafting.

5. An example of a finished pleached hedge.

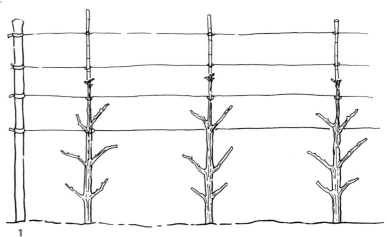

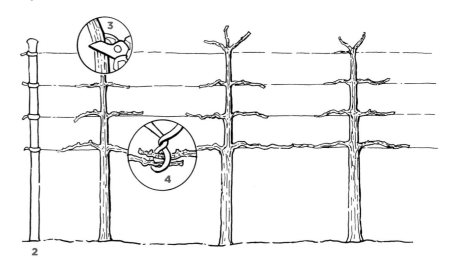

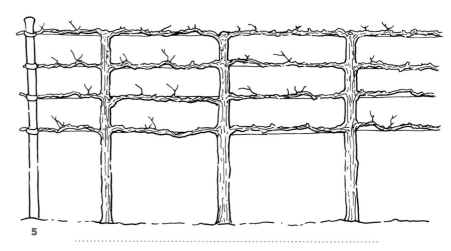

OPPOSITE, TOP: **Young branches of a newly pleached hedge.**
OPPOSITE, BOTTOM: **Newly laid hedge.**

ing more options for planting; and the air circulation is better, which in winter prevents frost from settling in. It is the aesthetic reasons behind them that really count though—the sculptural lines of the trunks and the strong horizontal of the bottom of the hedge offer more than a solid hedge can ever hope to.

Beyond the standard format, more unusual examples of pleaching are to be found in places like Plas Brondanw, the extraordinary garden of Clough Williams-Ellis in north Wales. One part of this garden is surrounded by lime trees, their branches plaited together in a chaotic, pretzel-like latticework. No parallel tiers or tensioned wire here, just the sense that one is looking at a thin cross section from the middle of a tree. I have seen something similar in Provence, where within the main frame of the crown of pollarded trees, smaller branches are knotted together, creating one organic mass rather than individual branches. Similarly, the plane trees (or sycamores, as they are known in North America) of Castillon are pleached to cover the roads of Provence with a criss-cross of branches, so that each tree is joined not only to those on either side, but to those opposite too. The effect is like that of bunting or Christmas lights, more decorative than functional, although it would also cast some shade on the road, like the pollarded planes of the area do.

The tradition of pleaching follows a similar pattern to the rural art of hedge laying. A chance meeting at a forestry show with a particularly earthy, fully bearded, backwoods type introduced me to the many different regional varieties of the laid hedge, but they all hinge around cutting down saplings within the hedge almost at ground level and laying the trunks flat, keeping a small bit of connecting wood and cambium layer

....

OPPOSITE, TOP, LEFT: **Unusual pleached trees in Castillon, Provence, France.** Photo by James Mitchell.
OPPOSITE, TOP, RIGHT: **Pleached hedge at Plas Brondanw in Anglesey, north Wales.** Photo by Charles Hawes.
OPPOSITE, BOTTOM: **An ash tree (Fraxinus excelsior) that was once part of a laid hedge.**

between the stump and the trunk. This way the sapling keeps growing, with new shoots emerging along its entire length that thicken up the hedge. A newly laid hedge is an extraordinary sight, and a certain amount of faith is needed to be sure it will continue to grow, but grow they do. Old trees in hedgerows that were once laid but have been allowed to grow away over the years develop characteristic bases where they once lay flat—strange, multi-stemmed trees growing along one dimension that seem to take on almost human qualities, with backs, necks and shoulders.

The tree sculptor Dan Ladd uses traditional techniques such as pleaching, laying and grafting in his work, noticeably in his Banister Trees project at the DeCordova Sculpture Park and Museum in Massachusetts, U.S.A, where 11 virus-resistant elm trees are being trained and grafted to form a living banister up a slope, allowed to grow away over the summer but pruned back to its framework each winter. Ladd's work recalls that of British sculptor David Nash, and in particular his Ash Tree Dome, which has been a work in progress for more than 30 years. A ring of young ash trees (*Fraxinus excelsior*) have been trained into a dome shape through pruning, spiraling around as they reach upwards. Directional pruning, more than training, has shaped the trees here by encouraging growth in a particular direction while removing the rest, so rather than smooth curves, there are a series of bends and kinks in Nash's work.

The modern alternative to rural hedge laying is agricultural flailing. Not everyone likes it, for environmental and aesthetic reasons, but I have rather a soft spot for it when done well. Man and (very big) machine working in perfect harmony. Visually, the way freshly cut hedges follow the contours of the landscape, undulating with the terrain, really excites me, but so too does the uncompromising nature of the method: as the tractor rumbles along, everything within its reach is ripped to shreds, with no sentimentality or concern involved. No stepping back to check, no uncertainty. Now *that* is pruning.

HEDGES AS SCULPTURE

During my research into hedges, I came across other ways of using them in the garden that do not fit into the more traditional categories. Veddw in south Wales, for example, makes use of beautiful wave-shaped yew hedges in a strikingly modern way by interlocking and overlapping yew plants to create a scene reminiscent of the stylized Hokkusai wave prints. The sense of depth is heightened by the repetition of receding contours, much like the surrounding landscape. The hedges are part of a formal pond area, creating bold reflections in the still water, but they also provide an organic, natural feel that draws one in, as enticing as the Welsh landscape itself.

At my mother's garden in Dorset, a similar result has been achieved with two short, undulating *Thuja plicata* hedges that separate the greenhouse from the rest of the garden. They are staggered, one a few feet back from the other, and overlapping, so from a distance it appears to be a solid hedge, but on approaching, the gap reveals itself. *Thuja* makes a good hedge—it is easy to dismiss as just another conifer, but it has richer, more vibrantly coloured foliage than many others, and also responds better to heavy pruning (not as well as yew, but much better than ×*Cupressocyparis leylandii*). Clipping it recently, I was reminded not only of what a magnificent, resinous smell the foliage has, but also of how important it is to clip the sides of any hedge properly, allowing for good batter.

Both this hedge and the ones at Veddw encourage the viewer to get involved with the space, to enter it rather than merely walk straight through. They hide and reveal, stretching the perceived space around them. It is a trick commonly used in Japanese gardens, where entrances rarely follow a straight path, but instead come to abrupt walls or hedges that force the visitor off at a right angle, slowing them down and focusing them. It also screens the view beyond without blocking it, so serves its purpose of privacy, while involving the viewer physically and mentally.

The evergreen azalea *karikomi* at Daichi-ji Temple in Shiga prefecture, Japan, uses the same interlocking and overlapping play of outlines as the yews at Veddw, although in a purely decorative way, one that is designed to be looked at rather than walked through. The tiered waves create the same sense of depth and movement, stretching the perspective and drawing us into the view.

The angle that a hedge is viewed from can make an enormous difference—the tall, maze-like cypress hedges in the Generalife gardens at the Alhambra in Granada, Spain, appear to echo the outlines of the buildings behind when seen from above, reminding one of the architectural role of hedges, with the sharp right angles and flat planes assuming an artificial, man-made character. Unfortunately, the state of these hedges also reminds us that ultimately cypresses are not the best long-term choice for hedges and topiary, as the bald patches attest.

Taking the idea of hedge as art a few steps further, Nicky Fraser and her maintenance business Knives Out, based in Shropshire, England, use the hedge as a blank canvas, carving 'graffiti' into the foliage. Cheeky, funky and, like a lot of graffiti, fleeting, it remains visible for only a short time, until the hedge has grown out. Some projects, MySpace for example, have become permanent, with Nicky carefully clipping out the letters each summer. Others have since faded back into the undergrowth, while others still (Anarchy is a favourite of mine) only existed on the day and were wiped out with a pair of shears before the job was finished.

Nicky's work raises an interesting point about the permanence of topiary—when seen as sculpture, it lies at the opposite end of the spectrum to established artists such as Ian Hamilton-Finlay, whose landscape and gar-

OPPOSITE, TOP: **The uncompromising nature of hedge flailing.**
OPPOSITE, BOTTOM, LEFT: **Dan Ladd's living sculpture Banister, a work in progress in Massachusetts, U.S.A.** Photo by Daniel Ladd.
OPPOSITE, BOTTOM, RIGHT: **David Nash's Ash Tree Dome.** Photo by David Nash.

den art, snippets of text carved into stone, evoke the past and a sense of eternal presence. Hedges and topiary appear to be the solid foundations of the garden, never changing, rock-like, but of course as plants they are continually growing and changing, being cut back and re-shaped over time. The role of the gardener here becomes much more assertive and influential, especially in pieces like Anarchy that exist only until the rest of the hedge or topiary has been finished, much like installations and art happenings that are fleeting and rely on the viewer and photographic evidence to give them substance.

That leads us on to the fascinating potential of gue-rilla pruning, the as yet undocumented pruning of trees, shrubs, and hedges in public spaces (or private ones, for militant exponents of the art). I have often passed potential targets that I felt were crying out for some attention, just asking for a quick going over with a pair of shears or some creative tweaking. Various practi-

cal and social considerations have always prevented me but I do not think of it as being particularly anti-social behavior. Overgrown highway embankments are where my imagination runs riot. Along sections of the major road that takes me to London, yew seems to have been a popular choice of the landscapers, a thoughtful and appropriate selection given the chalky soil in the area. The thousands of young yew plants there are now large bushes, some small trees, and all would make perfect lumps, bumps, *twmps* or other shapes.

....

PAGE 96: **The yew hedges at Veddw.** Photo by Charles Hawes.
PAGE 97: **The hedges at Alhambra, Granada, Spain.** Photo by Graeme Churchard.
OPPOSITE, TOP: **Undulating *Thuja plicata* hedge.**
OPPOSITE, BOTTOM: **Daichi-ji, Shiga, Japan.** Photo by Mark Fountain.
ABOVE: **MySpace and Graffiti by Nicky Fraser of Knives Out.** Photos by Danny Beath.

FOUR
Niwaki *and the Eastern Influence*

JAPAN IS WHERE MY INTEREST in pruning began, and also where my mind instinctively wanders when I think about trees, gardens, landscapes and pruning. My fascination with the latter started from an artistic point of view—I had just left art school in London and travelled to see the cherry blossoms in Kyoto, but I was initially interested more in the cultural aspect of these trees than their aesthetics. I stayed for a month on that trip, but was soon back, teaching English and working at a landscape nursery in rural Osaka. That was back in the 1990s. I now head back there whenever possible (my wife, Keiko, is Japanese, so luckily we have a good excuse) and each time I do, I am amazed and stimulated, as if experiencing it all for the first time, at the amount and intensity of pruning that goes on.

The journey from Kansai International Airport to Keiko's family home near a town called Tondabayashi in Osaka prefecture gets my creative juices flowing right from the start of each trip. I love seeing the Chinese junipers planted along the exit to a town called Kaizuka, also in Osaka prefecture (as a nice touch, *Juniperus chinensis* 'Kaizuka' has been chosen as the town tree) and the hilltop nursery I see from the road, nestled in amongst *Cryptomeria japonica* plantations. Each time I visit, I make a point of visiting a handful of temples, in Kyoto if possible, and travelling to a part of the country I have not yet been to, but I also spend as much time as possible exploring locally, walking through backstreets

of the neighbourhood and peeking into private gardens, always thrilled by what I find.

The Japanese prune for similar reasons to everyone else: to keep plants under control in the garden and on the streets, as well as for maximum yield and efficient use of space. What is different, though, is their overall aesthetic in the garden. Reduced down to their most basic principles, Japanese gardens can be seen as microcosms of nature that are inspired by the physical landscapes of the country itself: mountains, forests, waterfalls and rocky coastlines. It is these features that are reproduced, either literally or symbolically, in Japanese gardens, creating what I like to think of as an essence of the landscape.

Whereas in the West pruning tends to remove plants from their natural state, in Japan, the aim is to manipulate and enhance that natural state. Put simply, the traditions of European topiary involve man's order and control over nature, while in Japan, it is man working *with* nature, in producing or recreating a quintessential, idealized version of it. Perhaps this stems from religious differences, as unlike Christians, Buddhists tend to think of themselves as being a part of, rather than detached from, nature. Trees and shrubs are pruned and shaped as if to create caricatures of themselves, evoking the atmosphere associated with high mountains, dappled woodland glades, isolated trees battered by gales on a rocky cliff, or the majestic presence of a mature specimen.

We tend to describe topiary as the clipping of trees and shrubs into formal or playful shapes. When we do,

OPPOSITE: **Black pines (*Pinus thunbergii*) ready for sale at a nursery in Osaka, Japan.**

we think instinctively of the topiary gardens of Europe, England and North America. The Japanese also refer to topiary when describing these gardens, but when they refer to their naturally styled garden trees, they rarely call them much more than trees, or garden trees (*niwaki*). The very term garden tree implies that more often than not these specimens will have been grown, trained and pruned in relation to the scale and design of the garden, as opposed to trees that are allowed to grow freely in the wild.

In the past in the West, we have described these *niwaki* as bonsai, a term that appears to make sense but actually is incorrect—bonsai refers to the growing of trees on plates or pots, and is the art of miniaturization and root control as much as tree shaping. *Niwaki* in the garden are grown in the ground, not pots, and while some are miniaturized, many are enormous. The term cloud pruning is also sometimes used to describe *niwaki*, as us Westerners try to understand and categorize something that appears so alien to us, but nor is this altogether accurate either. Cloud pruning does, however, get the gist of the idea across, and seems to have been adopted as the general term to describe Japanese pruning generally in the West.

It is interesting to look at Japanese pruning and aesthetics on a worldwide scale, not just as an isolated phenomenon but as part of the bigger picture. Nor should this kind of pruning be considered unique to Japan. Gardeners in China and Korea (where much of Japanese culture stemmed from) use similar techniques, as do those in Thailand and beyond. The plants used and ensuing results vary from country to country (and

even within Japan itself, from region to region) but the underlying thought process and aesthetics share much common ground, appearing to be very similar to the uninitiated.

JAPAN

Gardens in Japan can be broken down into several core groups. Temple gardens, palaces, castles and parks are where the traditional art of the garden lies, as seen in books and witnessed by visitors to Kyoto. Within temple gardens in particular, there is an enormous variety of styles, including those of tea gardens, dry gardens, moss gardens and what people describe nowadays as zen gardens. Almost without exception, these various styles of Japanese gardens all contain examples of *niwaki* pruning, along with the other key ingredients of Japanese gardens: rocks and water.

The term zen was actually coined by an American, Lorraine Kuck, in her 1935 book, *One Hundred Gardens of Kyoto*, and only since then has it been adopted by the Japanese and considered a historical style. Shoji Yamada's fascinating book *Shots in the Dark* looks in great detail at how this myth of zen was propagated and distorted in the twentieth century, giving rise to the current notions held by many Japanese and non-Japanese alike, of the influence of zen in the garden. It is not for me to comment, but it raises interesting points about how opinion changes over time and how what we take for granted is not necessarily the only way of thinking.

Beyond these more familiar gardens, there are the millions of small, private ones all over the country, from contemporary city gardens to the informal yards of rural homes. These gardens share some of the aesthetics of the temples and palace gardens, but due to their size (most private gardens, especially in towns and cities where space is scarce, are small) the sense of scale is reduced. The landscape of Japan is still the underlying theme, but this can sometimes be reduced to no more than a few trees and a path as an approach to the house. Alongside the symbolism and the cultural associations

PAGE 102: **Local neighbourhoods in Japan have as much to offer as the temple gardens of Kyoto.**
PAGE 103: **The stylized perfection of a Japanese red pine (*Pinus densiflora*).**
OPPOSITE, TOP: **Korakuen in Okayama prefecture, one of the classic gardens of Japan.**
OPPOSITE, BOTTOM: **Private gardens are often no more than a few trees in the yard—in this case *Podocarpus macrophyllus* (left) and *Juniperus chinensis* 'Kaizuka' (right).**

that are linked to the art of the garden are the more basic necessities: privacy, shade and tranquility.

By looking briefly at the main styles and techniques of *niwaki*, I hope to introduce the idea that there are definite pruning links between the East and the West. Although pine pruning, azalea clipping and the training and shaping of evergreens might, at first sight, appear to be from another planet horticulturally, they are more closely related to hedge cutting, topiary and even fruit tree pruning practices than one might realize. Seeing rows of pines for sale at nurseries in Japan, it soon becomes clear that despite the artistry involved in their creation, they are still units, produced for a market, and are not all that different to the rows of formal standards for sale at European nurseries.

Karikomi

Karikomi translates roughly as 'clipped shapes' and is closely related to European-style box clipping, although irregular and organic shapes are favoured over the perfect symmetry of classical Europe. Mushrooms and donuts (or *anpan* and *nikuman*, if you are familiar with Japanese food) are the order of the day, hugging the ground like droplets of mercury. When planted en masse, it is known as *okarikomi*—the *o-* prefix here translates as large and usually involves a group of plants clipped into giant mounds and banks, like smooth rounded hills.

Some of my most favourite gardens of all are the temple gardens nestled in the foothills surrounding Kyoto. Shisendo-in is one, in the Higashiyama foothills, north east of the city. It is stacked full of *karikomi* azaleas— all shapes and sizes, including great banks of them that line a path down to its lower garden, like looming cliffs overhanging a ravine. Further down this path, in the lower clearing, lies a collection of blobs in an apparently haphazard arrangement, like boulders discarded by a passing glacier.

Another favourite of mine is the garden of Konpuku-ji, not far from Shisendo-in. The temple backs onto a slope that is covered in azaleas, ranging from wide, large blobs at the bottom to much smaller ones nearer the top. This variation helps add depth to what is actually quite a small garden: using low, wide shapes towards the front of the view, and smaller ones beyond gives the impression of dramatically receding distance, a sense that is added to by the use of the three-tiered hedge beyond that.

The extraordinary garden at the Adachi Museum in Shimane prefecture also has fine azalea *karikomi* blobs, vast mushrooms that lead the eye back through the view, creating a sense of perspective amongst the rocks and pines. In contrast to the scale and pristine quality of Adachi, most other gardens have a pocket of more relaxed *karikomi* tucked away somewhere. Tofuku-ji in Kyoto, for example, has a group of blobs acting as an informal backdrop to the famous chequerboard moss. Neither the *karikomi* nor the moss here ever seems to be in top shape, but in complete contrast to the Adachi Museum, that only adds to the character.

The influence of *karikomi* on modern Western gardening is plain to see. The use of the blob rather than the ball creates a more natural sense of the landscape rather than the artificial, man-made constructions of traditional European gardens. This has been adopted in turn by contemporary designers in the West and seems particularly popular in Belgium and Holland, often planted in clusters of varying sizes—blobberies is the technical term. They add the look and feel of traditional topiary, hinting at its weight and volume without the added baggage that comes with it, in a more natural context. They fit as comfortably into densely planted borders as they do in more contemporary, minimalist gardens.

....

OPPOSITE, TOP AND BOTTOM: *Karikomi* at Shisendo-in, **Kyoto, Japan.**
PAGE 108, TOP: **Konpuku-ji, Kyoto, Japan.**
PAGE 108, BOTTOM: **Adachi Museum, Japan.**
PAGE 109: **An informal garden of various blobs, Hakone, Kanagawa prefecture, Japan.**

Thinning

One area of Japanese pruning that seems to be largely overlooked by the rest of the world is that of thinning. The fact that it has not become widely incorporated into gardens in the West, like cloud pruning or *karikomi*, is not surprising, as it is far less tangible within a garden, but nevertheless it is an important part of the Japanese gardener's repertoire, with plenty to offer gardeners in the West.

In the *tsuboniwa* (small courtyard gardens) and especially the *roji* (tea gardens), thinned trees are used extensively to create dappled shade and the feel of woodland areas (the term *roji* can be translated as dewy path, conjuring up images of damp, mossy forests). In this technique, conifers such as pines, podocarps, as well as evergreens and deciduous trees are all pruned to preserve their natural form but still filter light through to the enclosed spaces.

Evergreen oaks and their relatives, such as *Quercus myrsinifolia*, *Q. acuta*, *Lithocarpus densiflorus* and *L. edulis*, as well as hollies such as *Ilex pedunculosa* and *I. integra* and other, better known shrubs (to Western gardeners, that is) such as *Aucuba japonica*, *Camellia japonica* and *Pieris japonica* are all heavily thinned in Japan (and often, to the uninitiated, appear overly so). The trunk and main branches are defined by removing surplus side branches and any clutter from within the tree: crossing or in-growing branches, dead twigs and old foliage—the usual suspects—and then thinning out any lesser branches that are growing too close together or too regularly.

Maintenance pruning is basically a continuation of the original formative pruning. It involves cutting back and thinning out of new growth, preserving the open structure by removing upward growing shoots and leaving those that grow outwards. Different species behave differently and some will produce epicormic growth around the trunk, which should be removed. In time, by cutting back to the same point each year, the branches start to develop bolls, much as pollarded trees do. This

effect is noticeable on some of the older, larger trees—the oaks in particular. If it is not wanted (although personally, I like it) the branch needs to be cut back to a point where a new side shoot can take its place. This is best done as part of a cycle, taking care not to replace too many branches at one time.

What is left ought to look natural, and this is one of the reasons why the importance of thinning has not been fully recognized outside of Japan—it is so hard to pin down, to photograph and to talk about, unlike the azalea *karikomi* for example, which is far more clear cut. The skill in thinning lies in covering one's tracks, leaving no footprints, making it one of the hardest techniques to do well. To Western eyes, Japanese gardens can be full of contradictions—the whole business of creating a garden inspired by a landscape, that is so labour intensive and ultimately artificial—and thinning might well be the biggest contradiction of them all.

Conifers such as *Cryptomeria japonica*, *Chamaecyparis obtusa*, *Chamaecyparis pisifera*, *Cedrus deodara* and to a lesser extent *Abies firma*, are also frequently thinned, often as very large trees. Their natural, spire-like forms and proportions are preserved, but again, as with the evergreens, their density is greatly reduced. Thinning gets rid of the old brown foliage that conifers collect within their branches, which in turn lets light into the body of the tree and allows regeneration within the branches rather than just from the tips.

Why bother with thinning in the garden? Well, if you are keen on evergreens, but find that they soon outgrow their position, thinning is another creative way to solve this problem. Raising, cutting back or clipping might be more obvious answers, but thinning does much to preserve the natural habit of the plant, lightening the load without drastic surgery and still preserving the overall outline of the plant. This technique can be particularly useful in smaller urban gardens, where space is at a premium but so too is privacy. Dense hedges provide privacy but can cast too much shade, while thinned shrubs have a more open feel to them, letting in more light but

also preserving their primary screening function. In a more natural-style garden, thinning can be the perfect solution, allowing you all the advantage of evergreens (including year-round foliage) without their somewhat overbearing presence (their enormous size often ensures that they will gradually take over the entire garden). Any plant can be thinned, although the results will vary depending on habit, leaf size and smaller details such as whether growth is alternate or opposite (a common practice is to remove one in each pair of opposite-growing branches to create a less intentional, symmetrical feel). Japanese levels of attention are not essential, although once one establishes a method and routine, nor are they inconceivable.

Pine pruning

Pines are the most important trees in the Japanese garden. Their pruning is an art unto itself, taking years to master. The three species native to Japan, *Pinus thunbergii* (black pine) *P. densiflora* (red pine) and *P. parviflora* (white pine) are all pruned in roughly the same way, although styles vary for different uses and from region to region. Some trees, where size, budget or time dictate, are only pruned once in the year, very heavily, in mid summer. Ideally, however, pruning is a twice-yearly affair, once in late spring or early summer, and then again in the autumn.

When pruning twice in the year, the first prune, known as *midoritsumi*, involves pinching out the new growth, often referred to as candling. By removing or cutting back this new growth, or candles, all the latent energy that would have been directed into that year's growth is instead checked, and later manifests itself as a second flush of much shorter, denser growth. There are all sorts of fine points to consider—how many to remove, how far back to remove them, whether to

remove more from the top of the tree than the bottom and exactly when to do it. Black pines are the most vigorous and are pruned the most heavily, with the entire candle being pinched out at the base. Red pines are less vigorous, so accordingly the candles are pinched out one or two inches (5 cm) from the base. The resulting second flush grows away over the summer (Japanese summers are very hot and humid—if you are trying this in cooler climes, lighter pruning might be called for) and by the autumn, the trees are dense, bushy and in need of more pruning.

The autumn prune, known as *momiage*, is basically a thinning process, removing the excess of the summer foliage and older needles to open up the branches and let light in. Light is vital because without it, new growth only appears on the outsides of the branches, making it hard to contain their size as they grow. The amount of thinning depends on the region and style, but typically the white pine is thinned the least, as it develops dense, solid branches, while black pines are generally thinned the most—sometimes too much so for Western sensibilities.

October and November are great months to be in Japan—everywhere one goes, there are gardeners up ladders, thinning the pines. A walk around the suburbs or rural areas offers plenty of opportunity to talk to them or take photos. *Sumimasen - shashin totte ii desuka*? (Excuse me, can I take a photo?) usually works. On our most recent trip to Japan, while staying at Keiko's brother's home in a village called Sabi, in Osaka prefecture, I took an early morning walk around the village, and saw a small truck, laden down with tripod ladders, pull into a driveway. I lingered and watched as two men got out, unloaded the ladders, tied white towels around their heads, drank canned coffee and smoked cigarettes—the usual preparation for a manual day's work all over Japan. This was before eight o'clock, and I decided to leave them to it, but come back later to take photos. On my return, the younger of the two was clipping a *Podocarpus macrophyllus*, while the other, more expe-

rienced gardener, was thinning a black pine. They saw me watching from across the road and called me over, taking the time to chat (my Japanese is not great, but I have had a good bit of practice in these situations). Of course, this being rural Japan, they knew my brother-in-law, who by chance appeared five minutes later to help explain this strange foreigner who was so interested in their daily work.

Branch training

The idea that the essence of a tree can be imposed artificially, rather than achieved naturally through time, is fundamental to Japanese *niwaki*. A lot of the magic that seems to go into them is not actually in the pruning, but in their earlier, formative training in the nurseries. There are countless techniques, varying from region to region and species to species, but the basic idea of training branches lies at the root of many of them. Depending on the style of tree, horizontal branches give the impression of the maturity that defines large, old trees growing in the wild—their branches tend to be weighed down by their own weight, eventually naturally assuming a stretched out, horizontal shape.

On the smaller, more artificial scale of *niwaki*, a helping hand is needed. From a young age, side branches can be trained down using splints and rope, much like fruit trees and pleached hedges are trained in the West.

....

PAGE 114: *Pinus parviflora* is usually pruned in a denser style than other pines.
PAGE 115, TOP TWO PHOTOS: Annual pruning needs to be heavy enough to last the whole year. *Pinus thunbergii*, before and after, Yamagata prefecture, Japan. Photos by Yasuhito Tobitsuka.
PAGE 115, BOTTOM TWO PHOTOS: *Midoritsumi*, pinching out the new growth in early summer. *Pinus radiata*, not a pine usually associated with Japanese pruning, England.
OPPOSITE, TOP TWO PHOTOS: Recently pruned *Pinus thunbergii* in a nursery and a private garden, Osaka prefecture, Japan.
OPPOSITE, BOTTOM, LEFT: *Sumimasen - shashin totte ii desuka?* Gardeners at work, Osaka prefecture, Japan.
OPPOSITE, BOTTOM, RIGHT: Autumn pine pruning, Nara prefecture, Japan.

There is a small degree of science involved here, to do with auxins and growth patterns, but I doubt that the average Japanese nurseryman is interested in that—it is the nitty gritty that concerns them, and us.

Young branches are easily trained into place by tying them down with string, usually securing it to the trunk below. Japanese gardeners use *shuronawa*, which is string woven from the hairy trunks of trachycarpus palms, but any kind will do, though preferably one made of natural fibres. Notice how tying your string at different points along the branch will bend the branch in different ways—tie it too near the end of the branch and just the tip will be trained down, rather than the whole branch.

Larger branches need a bamboo splint to help them on their way. Simply tie a stout cane along the whole length of the branch, so that the cane reaches slightly beyond the central trunk, then train the splinted branch down as described above. In some cases, surprisingly thick branches of older trees can also be retrained, sometimes in situ in the garden, but more often at a nursery. The process is a highly sculptural one, as the branches are wrapped with rope to provide a splint-like casing to prevent damage. Posts are then propped up underneath the wrapped branches to provide resistance as they are gradually trained down using a pulley system. One variation of this technique involves intentionally cracking the bark of the branch to allow more movement, and then re-setting it over time—not a job for the faint hearted. Interestingly, the rural European tradition of hedge laying relies on a similar technique, that of cutting the trunks of young saplings, before laying the trunks down along the ground for new growth to shoot from.

Within the garden, a more gradual training of branches can be achieved by pruning alone. In these cases, the branch is directed not by ropes or splints, but by selective pruning, removing the main leader of a branch and encouraging the lower lateral to continue. Of course, the very act of pruning works against the

HOW TO TRAIN SIDE BRANCHES

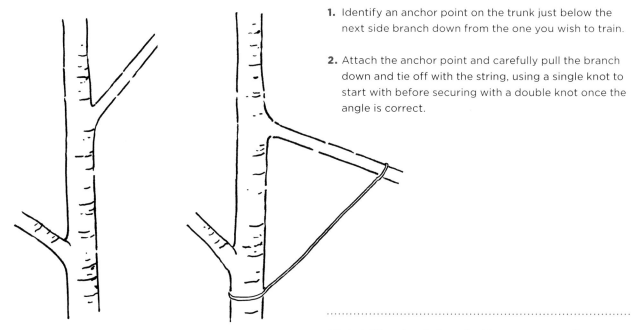

1. Identify an anchor point on the trunk just below the next side branch down from the one you wish to train.

2. Attach the anchor point and carefully pull the branch down and tie off with the string, using a single knot to start with before securing with a double knot once the angle is correct.

BELOW: **Wrapping the branch with rope acts as a splint.** Photo by Edzard Teubert.
OPPOSITE: **Training a pine in Japan.** Photo by Edzard Teubert.

training process, as it lightens the branch and prevents its weight from holding it down. This is another great contradiction of pruning—attempts to reproduce natural forms are constantly at odds with nature itself.

Branch training is taken to its limit in styles such as *monkaburi* (*mon*, meaning gate and *kaburi*, from the verb *kaburu*, meaning to wear or put on) when one branch from a tree (usually a pine or *Podocarpus macrophyllus*) is trained over the gateway or driveway of a home. It is a standard motif of domestic gardens and is a common sight in traditional residential areas.

A similar technique is also seen in temple gardens, when a lower branch is trained out along a path, supported on posts as it gets longer and longer. Elsewhere, branches are trained to hang over lanterns, or extend out over water. One of my favorites is a red pine branch that is trained around the borders of a private garden in Kyoto. It makes a right angle bend as it turns the corner of the wall and continues on its way. Sometimes it seems that branches are extended on a whim, with single branches making a beeline for a particular point, or at other times meandering casually across an open area. What is interesting about these—apart from the initially bizarre sight of a horizontally growing tree—is the work-in-progress branches one comes across. Even in temple gardens, work on these is never completed, and it is quite common to find a 12 in. (30 cm) flush of vertical growth at the end of one of these horizontal branches that has been allowed to grow away, before being tied down that winter to elongate the branch.

Branch training need not be reserved solely for authentic *niwaki* work—it can also be used to add character to various other projects, for example blocking or creating views. It is also a great way to add spread to mushroom-shaped standards and parasol shapes,

speeding up the gradual process of sideways expansion. As already pointed out, the techniques and results of branch training are similar to that of fruit training, and are well within the grasp of most gardeners.

Tamazukuri

Having looked at clipped azaleas and thinned trees, another popular technique in Japan is a combination of the two—clipped trees, or *tamazukuri*. *Zukuri* translates as style, and *tama* as round, so it loosely covers a wide range of trees and shapes, from the small *Ilex crenata* cloud trees that are exported to Europe from Japan (but are noticeably absent from many gardens in Japan) right up to the enormous clipped junipers and podocarps. These kinds of trees are quicker to produce, easier to maintain and cheaper than pines, so they tend to be used more in private gardens, often as screens in front of the house.

The term *tamazukuri* does not describe in enough detail all the possible varieties of shapes and sizes one sees in Japan. Trunks can be straight or curved, branches trained or untrained, trees clipped into balls, blobs, flat tops and flat bottoms. Branches can be long or short, and tightly spaced so the tree is almost solid, or well spaced so that the outline of each branch is clear. Evergreens and conifers are both commonly used here, deciduous ones only rarely.

There are three ways to produce this sort of tree, though these techniques are not all entirely Japanese in their origin. One can either start from scratch with a young plant, or with an established, bushy plant, or with a mature, overgrown one. I would describe the first option as similar to a sculptor modelling with clay, the second as carving in stone and the third as a combination of the two. With all three approaches, as there are so many possibilities, it is a good idea to decide roughly what branch length and density is required right from the start, although this need not be set in stone, as often plans change midway through a project. Generally speaking, a non-symmetrical look is favoured, with

....

OPPOSITE, TOP: *Pinus thunbergii* trained in the *monkaburi* style over a gateway.
OPPOSITE, BOTTOM: *Pinus thunbergii* trained over water at Korakuen, Okayama prefecture, Japan.

an intentionally natural feel to the branch spacing—not directly opposite, or arranged in regular tiers like those seen on wedding cakes.

The first technique, starting from scratch, involves thinning and shaping the branches as they grow, making decisions each year and only pruning the top when the plant is the right height.

New projects can even be planted at an angle and then trained back on themselves, to get a good bend low down. The trick with training the trunk is to keep it natural looking and irregular—Japanese trees always try to blend in rather than stand out (although in China, they tend to be more overtly bendy, in a more ornamental way). Ideally, side branches should grow from the outside of a bend, not the inside, as the natural flow of energy is stronger here, like the flow of a meandering river. The disadvantage of starting with a young plant is that one is restricted by its growth rate. Even though the branches might seem well developed, it will take some time before the trunk reaches any sense of maturity.

The second technique is the quickest and easiest, but requires a certain leap of faith. Established, bushy shrubs that have already reached the right height and filled out a bit are perfect.

If working on a conifer other than yew, take care not to cut back too hard into the branches that you keep, as they will not re-sprout from old wood. Yew and evergreens are more forgiving, and should re-sprout from whatever point you cut them to. Do not be worried about changing your mind—the plant may well steer you in a different direction than your original plan, or perhaps you have just returned from a trip to Kyoto, full of exciting plans for your garden—plants are forgiving and will soon cover up any miscalculations. Twice-yearly clipping will soon produce a strong, well-defined plant that is full of character. Pay attention to the space between branches, as these negative spaces can be its

OPPOSITE: **Branch of *Pinus densifora* trained along a path at Shokado, Kyoto, Japan.**

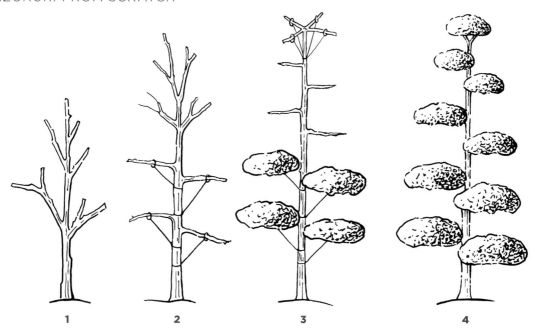

1 **2** **3** **4**

1. Choose a young shrub. As its trunk will be young and malleable, you may wish to either train the leader using a cane, or gradually introduce bends or kinks into the trunk using stakes, if desired.

2. Remove any unwanted branches and train down the remaining ones with twine if necessary.

3. Continue to train new branches down and begin to consolidate the lower ones through pruning. Clipping with hand-held topiary clippers will soon thicken up the foliage on the branches, and decisions about branch shape can then be made. Forming the head, the final tier of the tree, involves cutting the leader and training down its side branches the whole way around the stem, creating a parachute effect. This is then treated like any other side branch and gradually clipped into shape.

4. A finished example of the *tamazukuri* form.

strongest feature—keep the edges crisp and clean out any dead twigs on the inside that might be visible.

In the average garden, this second approach is the one I recommend: it uses plants that are already there, often solving the problem of what to do with them as they start to outgrow their usefulness. The results are pretty quick too—within a couple of years you will find that you no longer need to explain what is going on to guests, as the plant's shape becomes more obvious. Soon after that, you will start to become proud of your work and actually point it out to your guests, before looking

around the garden for your next project. The main disadvantage of this technique is that you have little control over the trunk, so you get what you are given, so to speak. This is fine if the finished tree is dense, but sometimes in a more open tree, a trunk that has been allowed to grow freely in the garden for years can be overly straight, with vertical side branches, and can end up looking disproportionate as an overall picture.

The final technique for producing *tamazukuri*-style trees is the most ambitious and ultimately most rewarding of all three. As part of the *fukinaoshi* process, which translates roughly as 're do', big old trees and shrubs are severely cut back (sometimes right down to the trunk) and allowed to re-grow from the old wood.

OPPOSITE: *Tamazukuri Chamaecyparis obtusa* 'Breviramea'.

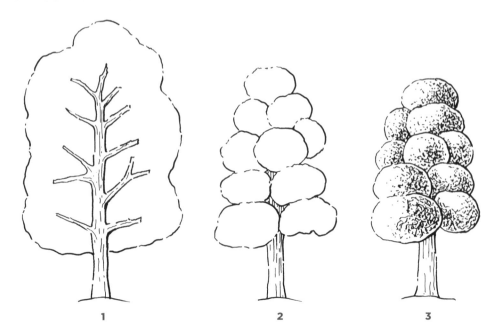

1   2   3

1. Look at the shrub and assess its branch pattern, peering inside it and pulling branches apart if necessary. Think about the overall shape you would like the plant to have, as well as how far apart you want the branches to be—this will obviously effect how many you will remove later.

2. Begin carving into the plant, using shears and secateurs to rough out the beginnings of a hidden shape. For a fully dense shape, you might not remove any branches at all, but treat the whole plant as one continuous surface. For a more open look, thin out any branches that are too close together. Later that year, or after the next growing season, go back over your plant with a pair of shears or topiary clippers to consolidate the new growth.

3. A final, finished *tamazukuri*.

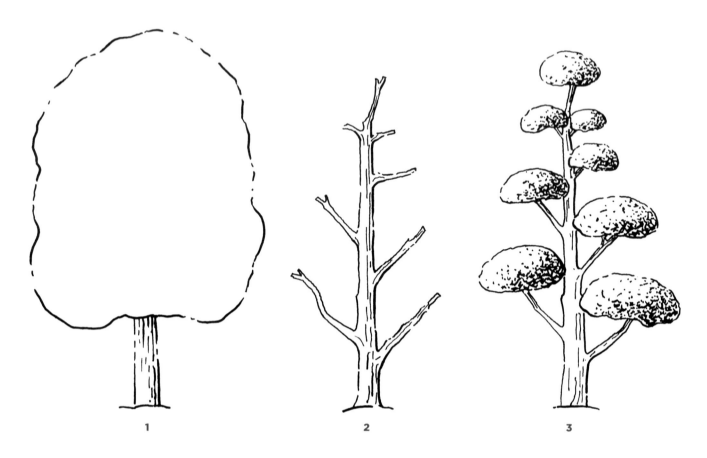

1

2

3

1. Select an old, established tree.

2. Cut back the foliage right down to the trunk and main branches.

3. Allow new growth to form, which is then trained and clipped back into rounded shapes.

OPPOSITE: **Starting with an established shrub.** *Osmanthus ×burkwoodii* **being carved into using the** *fukinaoshi* **process.**

The advantage of this technique is that you get the established trunk of a far more substantial tree, but reduce the overall size of the plant. In Japanese gardens, *niwaki* are often noticeable for having far wider trunks than their height would naturally dictate, as these proportions are more in keeping with the mature trees they emulate. Also, *fukinaoshi* is a great way of using plants in the garden that might otherwise be ready for the chop. Reducing the overall volume of the tree allows valuable light and space into the garden, as well as providing new focus to the area it inhabits.

The disadvantage of *fukinaoshi* in the garden is that for a year or so, you will have an unsightly—almost bald—tree to look at. At the nursery and in some work-in-progress gardens that is fine, but it is not for everyone. Worse still, just occasionally, hard pruning may get the better of the tree, and it will not recover, although this only really happens to old, tired trees that were near their end anyway.

So, I hope to have outlined just a few of the more common styles of Japanese pruning. For tree enthusiasts in general, Japan is a fascinating country to visit—there is not just an enormous range of trees there, but also a deep respect for very big and very old ones, whether in shrines and temples, deep in the mountains or even in crowded cities. One rather touching example of this reverence is a tree I came across in Tokyo that constantly wrestles with modern urban life. This old camphor tree (*Cinnamomum camphora*) is growing on a street that was having some construction work done on it. The tree was initially cut down, its stump to be ground out, but before building work commenced, the cut trunk started sending out suckers, like a coppiced tree. It was saved, and as a mark of respect was designated a sacred Shinto shrine. It is now a large, multi-stemmed tree, regally roped off with the *shimenawa*, or rope, and festooned with the folded paper *gohei* of the Shinto faith.

In temples and shrines one frequently comes across colossal old trees—ginkgos are a favorite—whose age and size are celebrated. These trees are often in a fairly poor state and on their last legs, but occasionally one also comes across extraordinary pines that have been pruned for hundreds of years and, through their pruning, are in fine health. The famous ship pine in the grounds of Kinkaku-ji, the Golden Pavilion, in Kyoto, is one such example. This *Pinus parviflora* has a lower branch that has been trained out over a trellis, supposedly resembling the prow of a ship. Photographs from the early twentieth century show the same tree pruned into a more deliberate shape, the prow very much a prow, with the upper branches trained over disc-shaped frames. It is exciting enough to compare the tree's growth over the best part of a century, but it is even more remarkable when one learns that the tree was originally a bonsai that was planted in its current resting place some 650 years ago.

Another white pine, this one at Hosen-in, also in Kyoto, has been pruned into a vast, Mt Fuji-like mound, visible amongst the flowering cherries. This one is also over 600 years old and is quite a sight, especially when viewed from inside the temple, looking from within its canopy at the various posts of cedar trunk used as crutches to support the weight of the tree above. Any tree this old is bound to be awe inspiring, but ones that have been constantly overseen and managed by man have an extra dimension and layer of character to them, which I find particularly fascinating.

PAGE 128: **A Shinto shrine around an old camphor tree in downtown Tokyo.**
PAGE 129: **Two views of the *Pinus parviflora* ship pine at Kinkaku-ji, Kyoto, Japan.** Photos permission of the Nagasaki University library and Solsken Design.
OPPOSITE, TOP AND BOTTOM: ***Pinus parviflora* at Hosen-in, Kyoto, Japan.** Photos by Alex Ramsay.

CHINA, SOUTH KOREA AND THAILAND

Japan's neighbours, China and South Korea, also prune their garden trees, but not always so intensely or determinedly. The results can sometimes appear more playful, quirky and decorative than in Japan, but to the uninitiated it could all be grouped together as an Eastern style. Similar pruning goes on in Thailand too, but in my enthusiasm for getting to Japan, I have never managed to stop off on the way and thus have never seen the well known trees outside the Royal Palace in Bangkok. The Thai take on pruning looks similar to the Japanese *tamazukuri*-style at first glance, but on closer inspection it is more ornamental and less about landscape. There is less emphasis on branch training, with the results being more pom-pom or poodle than one sees in Japan. The overall effect is fantastic—a magical jubilance that complements the atmosphere and the ornate architecture of the palace, so different to that of the temples or palaces in Kyoto. According to a friend from Thailand, Noi Rittirat, the trees are a mixture of *Streblus asper*, species of *Ficus* and *Tamarindus indica*, although Noi did say that identifying trees in Thailand is tricky because there is a tendency to use local common names rather than botanical ones.

CALIFORNIA

For lovers of tree pruning, virtually every garden in Japan is a fascinating experience, but what I find interesting about the techniques used is not so much the results within Japan, but what happens when they are used in the West, beyond Japanese-style gardens. I am more interested in applying the Japanese spirit of pruning to a whole range of plants and using the techniques as and when I feel appropriate, like adding a *karikomi* feel to box clipping, for example, or using *tamazukuri*-style trees as focal points in English borders, rather than more traditional yew topiary.

One part of the world that seems to have embraced Japanese pruning more than any other is California. It took me a while to realize why, but the reason is obvious—many Japanese immigrants to the United States settled in cities like Los Angeles in the first half of the twentieth century, and made landscape gardening their trade. After looking into it more deeply, I discovered the Southern California Gardeners' Federation and their interesting publication *Green Makers: Japanese American Gardeners in Southern California*. I read it hoping for information on pruning, but in fact it is more about the lives of the immigrant gardeners and how they coped in their new environment.

Arriving in California in the 1920s and 30s, work was hard to find. Despite not being professional gardeners back home, many Japanese arrivals developed a reputation for good, honest, hard, gardening work. This was usually regular maintenance—mainly mowing—but inevitably, when it came to pruning, the gardeners looked back East for inspiration. Although they were generally not trained, it seems these people figured out the rudiments of their native techniques and from there, over time, developed a style that though clearly Japanese in origin, owes as much to the Californian suburbs. Looking at it now, I like to think there is a definite Californian-Japanese fusion of styles going on the whole way up the Californian coast to San Francisco that occupies a unique position in the world of creative topiary.

Partly defined by its setting—in suburban California, most trees seem to sit close to the house, with a lawn in front of them, as features of a garden rather than an integral part of the design—this Californian take on *niwaki* owes much to the clear blue skies and simple, clean lines of the architecture in the area. Shapes here

OPPOSITE, TOP: **The Royal Palace, Bangkok, Thailand. Photo by Roy Lathwell.**
OPPOSITE, BOTTOM, LEFT: **A thinned *Pinus radiata* opens up the view. Photo by Ted Kipping, Tree Shapers.**
OPPOSITE, BOTTOM, RIGHT: ***Cupressus macrocarpa*—East meets West. Photo by Ted Kipping, Tree Shapers.**

OPPOSITE: **Californian *tamazukuri*.** Photo by David Martinez/ Dig It.
ABOVE: ***Olea europaea*, before and after.** Photos by Ted Kipping, Tree Shapers.

tend to be stronger and more sculptural than in Japan, casting strong shadows against the walls behind them in the bright sun.

California also has more than its fair share of Japanese-style gardens (I use the word style here because for me, a Japanese garden really has to be in Japan, and tended by Japanese gardeners, to be truly Japanese), some of which have interesting examples of pruning. The one in San Francisco's Golden Gate Park carries the Japanese-Californian fusion badge well, with some very authentic pines, as well as a good number of *tamazukuri*-style junipers verging more to the Californian side. Personally—and I will probably be shot for this—I feel that the residential gardens of the Californian suburbs have much more to offer than the larger Japanese-style gardens, however authentic and well done they are. Having seen countless gardens in Japan, I have seen very few foreign imitations that quite lived up to their aspirations. Outside of their native country, to me *niwaki* seem more interesting when removed from their native context and placed in the real world.

However, California also does a good line in all sorts of decorative pruning, not just of the Japanese variety. My own experiences are limited to San Francisco and the Bay Area, where I was constantly impressed by the amount of pruning I saw: the pollarded plane trees, the multi-stemmed eucalyptus and the rows of neatly clipped, lollipop street trees all define the city for me, along with the sheer variety of trees, in particular evergreens, on offer. It seems likely that this enthusiasm for pruning sprang from the early Japanese gardeners, but it is now being carried forward by the likes of Ted Kipping's Tree Shapers business in the Bay Area.

Tree Shapers work on the scale of tree surgeons and arboriculturists, but with the vision and attention to detail of artists. Their work includes raising, thinning and shaping the crowns of native trees such as the Monterey pine and cypress (*Pinus radiata* and *Cupressus macrocarpa*), solving the problems that large trees can cause—usually loss of light and views—in a creative and attractive way. Both these trees play an important part in the natural landscape of the California coast, being native to the Monterey Peninsula, but they are also an integral part of the man-made landscape. As the trees get bigger and the space around them gets smaller, it is this kind of creative pruning that prevents them becoming a social and structural problem.

EUROPE

Europe has only really embraced *niwaki* pruning quite recently. The British tradition of making Japanese-style gardens in the early twentieth century chose to ignore tree pruning in favour of plant collections, avidly planting the latest introductions and varieties. Not surprisingly, the more tangible elements of the Japanese garden were picked up on—rocks, water and ornaments such as lanterns, bridges and pagodas, but it was not until the nursery businesses on the Continent started importing trees from Japan that people really became aware of *niwaki*. Japanese small leaved holly (*Ilex crenata*) is the most common of the imports, but pines and Japanese yew (*Taxus cuspidata*) are also popular. The practicalities of importing trees (shipped over in refrigerated containers, or 20 or 40 ft. reefers, as they are known) limit the size and styles available. As a result, the range on offer in Europe has become fairly predictable, and does not reflect the true selection available in Japan.

What these imports have done, however, is to inspire gardeners and nurseries to grow their own, with some very interesting results. Always on for a bit of experimentation, the British nursery Architectural Plants, in Sussex, grow interesting orange barked myrtles (*Myrtus apiculata)* and the olive-relative *Phillyrea latifolia*. The myrtle, in particular, is a lovely contradiction—a native of South America, grown in England, in a Japanese-style. It has a lot to offer too, with its downy orange

OPPOSITE: **Cloud pruned hornbeams (*Carpinus betulus*) in Tom Stuart-Smith's 2008 RHS Chelsea garden.** Photo by Lesley Powell.

bark and dense, white flowers. Interestingly, this plant would never have been created in Japan, where *niwaki* are almost entirely native species, and exotics are only ever used in Western style gardens, where of course there is no *niwaki* pruning involved.

Back on the Continent, nurseries in Belgium and Germany produce cloud pruned hornbeam *niwaki* (*Carpinus betulus*), as made famous by Tom Stuart-Smith in one of his many gold medal gardens at the RHS Chelsea Flower Show. These are an interesting phenomena, being not only deciduous—which is relatively unusual for topiary of any form—but also native to Europe, as opposed to Japan. Although they bear little in common with genuine Japanese *niwaki* (intentionally so—Stuart-Smith could have gone for a far more Japanese feel, but that was not his plan), the use of native trees in his garden is closer in spirit to the true *niwaki* (traditionally Japanese natives) than many other choices. In Tom Stuart-Smith's uniquely English gardens, what better than native hornbeams?

Nurseries in Italy and Spain have also started producing *niwaki*-styled olive trees—enormous old trees grubbed out of olive groves, cut back hard (à la *fuki-naoshi* process) and pruned into shape. The results are rather bizarre, and as far removed from the natural (messy) habit of the olive as is possible, but with the character of their vast trunks, they make imposing and stylish alternatives. Olives are one of the toughest and most resilient types of tree, responding well to heavy pruning and transplanting, and as such are perfect material for *niwaki* treatment. They do, however, produce a fair amount of epicormic growth, and I would imagine trees like this require constant maintenance to stop them reverting back to their shaggy selves.

....

OPPOSITE, TOP: **A rare example of authentic Japanese-style pruning on Scots pines (*Pinus sylvestris*) in Peter Sievert's garden in Enfield, London, England.**
OPPOSITE, BOTTOM: ***Niwaki*-style *Olea europaea* at the Solitair nursery, Belgium. Photo by NV Solitair.**

FIVE
Decorative Tree Pruning

FUNNY WORDS LIKE POLLARD and pleach, fancy foreign ones like espalier, and slightly rude sounding ones like stool—they might sound old-fashioned, or overly grand for the average garden these days, but in fact the various elements of tree pruning are alive and well in today's gardens, large and small, rural and urban. Fruit tree pruning, street tree maintenance, traditional woodcrafts and various aspects of everyday horticulture all combine to make this oft overlooked area of pruning full of creative potential.

From a practical point of view, it entails good, sensible stuff like keeping trees to a certain size, creating or removing shade and masking or revealing views, but it also adds character and style, can evoke far off places, brings a touch of architecture and a great deal of style into the garden.

POLLARDING

Pollarding is the regular cutting back of growth from a certain point up a tree—you may have seen it in France, where they remain the keenest of pollarders, but look closely and it pops up everywhere. It takes two main forms, most apparent in winter, once any new growth has been removed: the classic shape is the open goblet style, a stag's antlers of branches propelling out from the main trunk. The more elemental shape is the drumstick, which has no side branches at all, just one great knob. Common to all established pollards are the bolls, the swollen lumps at the end of each branch (or the trunk)

OPPOSITE: *Cryptomeria japonica* var. *radicans* grown in the *daisugi* style.

where the tree's tissues have regenerated year after year. The Japanese name for pollarding is *kobushishi-tate*, which translates as fist pruning. Roll your sleeve up, clench your fist and you will understand.

Pollarding seems to have begun a long time back, predominantly as a source of firewood. Ancient woodlands in the UK were pollarded before the Norman invasion of 1066 in a managed system, which gave commoners wood gathering rights. The advantage of pollarding over chopping down a tree outright was that the tree remained living—always a good thing—while a renewable source of timber (relatively young growth that was not too heavy or required too much work to process) was constantly available. Trees were cut above animal grazing height, typically around the 6–7 ft. (2.0 m) mark and were recut over a regular cycle of up to 14 years. Woodland species included oak, lime, ash (the best source of firewood, as it burns happily while still green) hornbeam and beech—most of the common native hardwoods, in fact.

It is thought that ancient woodlands in populated areas were made up almost entirely of pollarded trees, such was the demand for firewood and timber. The idea of magnificent, mature trees covering the English landscape is something of a myth. Epping forest, north of London, is a fine example of how intensely managed woodland used to be: until 1878 there were something like 500,000 pollards throughout the forest, at a density of 390 to 740 trees per hectare (about 2.5 acres). Nowadays, with a new pollarding regime in order, the number is more like 50,000, still the highest number of pollards in any UK woodland. Interestingly, an act of Parliament was passed in England in 1698 banning the pollarding of oaks, as straight trunks were needed for shipbuilding, which must have reduced the number of pollards considerably.

Early woodland pollarding would have been purely functional, but as the craft turned into an art, pollarded trees started appearing in gardens for their visual appeal, not the raw materials they had to offer. Continental Europe is the home of the ornamental pollard, where they are variously used as street trees, shade trees, boundary trees and formal avenue trees. Plane trees (*Platanus ×hispanica*) and, especially further north, species of limes (*Tilia*) are the tree of choice. With foraging livestock not a threat and practical considerations such as harvesting being less of an issue, the traditional dimensions of the woodland are no longer necessary, and a different set of practical and aesthetic considerations are applied to pollarding instead.

Street trees are often pollarded to restrict their size, and out of necessity these trees are pruned heavily and quickly. The planes of London, for example, can sometimes be cut quite brutally, but when done well the result is fantastic, with whole streets lined with coral-like sculptures reaching up to the clean air above the busy streets. They do provoke objections though—the arguments against pruning in general are perhaps strongest when it comes to street pollarding. However, I would point out that expecting trees in a city to be natural is slightly missing the point, especially when one considers that so little of our rural landscape is natural anyway, let alone the urban landscape. As for the people who cry 'cruel' at the sight of pollarding, or any pruning for that matter—grow up, and lay off the Roald Dahl.

The sheer size of London's pollards make them an unrealistic source of inspiration for most gardens, but head to the Continent, especially France where pollarding seems to be a part of the national identity, and you will find examples on a much more inspiring scale. The

OPPOSITE: **Ancient beech (*Fagus sylvatica*) pollards in Epping forest.**

further south you go and the hotter it gets, the more you will see. Towns have their pollard-lined streets, but the squares and even carparks have them too, where they provide shade in the searing heat, offering some respite for shoppers and old men with their boules and pastis.

Get as far down France as Provence, and the pollard becomes a part of the landscape. Imposing mulberries lurk in rural gardens, their dark bark and straight, squat trunks supporting dense bushy growth in the summer, cut back to a scarred framework each winter. It is the plane trees here that really catch the eye though. One old tree I saw, while driving around Provence (we were on our way to Vaucluse, I remember, and Keiko, a keen partner in the delights of Provence, but a reluctant tree gazer, had her patience tested with yet another unscheduled stop) shaded the yard of a farmhouse. It was colossal, its trunk and branches bleached white, like the skeleton of an enormous, prehistoric mammal. It was the widest spreading pollard I have ever seen, on par with the pines one comes across in Japan that are trained out over trellises in temple grounds, going on and on with apparently no end in sight. It must have shaded generations of the same family, and keep them busy come pollarding time. I once saw a film, an old black and white one—I forget its title—where Foreign Legionnaires stationed somewhere in the Mediterranean, pollarded a plane tree by climbing up inside it and slashing away with machetes. Having seen this tree, I realized that the machete is a far more appropriate tool than secateurs for pruning on this scale, especially when the aesthetic result comes not from delicate, artful decisions but the overall effect.

Across the Atlantic, pollarding seems less common. You really have to get the whole way over to California to rediscover its delights. San Francisco is my favou-

rite city in the U.S.A., maybe even in the world, largely down to its remarkable collection of trees (and its European feel, its diverse culture, the amazing landscape of that part of California, the food, the hills, the sea lions . . .) Many of the trees here are left to grow freely, but there is also a good deal of pruning going on, including pollarding.

Most striking is the formal grid of plane trees in front of San Francisco's City Hall. Straight rows of trees are exciting enough as it is, grids of them even more so, but grids of these organic, silhouetted knuckles are another thing altogether. It was here that Donald Sutherland, in the film *Invasion of the Body Snatchers*, lets on at the end that he too has been snatched, giving out a terrifying roar with those trees behind him. Interestingly Mike Sullivan, in his excellent book *The Trees of San Francisco*, mentions that plane trees do not do very well in San Francisco's windy, foggy environment. (Mike, I should point out, is a tree lover in the true sense, with very little time for pruning—not that that should tarnish him in any way).

How to pollard

Pollarding is one of the most straightforward pruning jobs there is. Only one or two decisions need making, as the tree does most of the work and timing is largely irrelevant. If speed is of the essence and money no object, whole avenues of ready-grown pollards are available for sale at nurseries these days, but for best results, start young and do it yourself. A light standard (grown on a nursery to 10 ft. (3 m) with a clear trunk to about 6 ft. (1.8 m) or feathered whip (typically 8 ft. (2.4 m) with branches the whole way up the trunk) from the nursery is best, ideally with a straight trunk, so avoid those with a strong kink or a split leader. Decide what height you want the tree to grow to—there are no rules, only practical and aesthetic considerations, but plan for a clear trunk of 7 ft. (2.1 m), so even the tallest of us can move around freely underneath. You'll need a good spacing of branches around the tree, ideally three to five

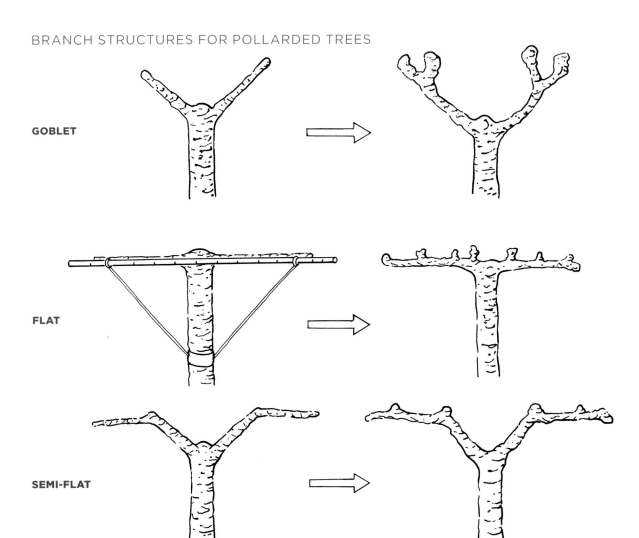

GOBLET

FLAT

SEMI-FLAT

Ideally, there will be a set of side branches on your tree roughly at the 7 ft or so mark, and above them is where you should make your first cut of many, using either secateurs or a saw. If your 7 ft. mark is between flushes of branches, you can encourage branches to grow at this point by cutting the sides of the leader to force new shoots out which will later become side branches, although there are normally suitable branches close enough that this is not necessary.

The next decision is whether you would like angled, goblet-shaped branches, or totally flat, horizontal ones. If you decide on the flat look, now is the time to start training them. The simplest way is to tie down each branch, using the trunk to tie the string to. Alternatively, you can create splints and trestles to train the branches to, but this seems unnecessary to me, and soon falls apart unless done well. Appreciate that not all branches

will train fully flat, and there is no point in forcing them, but what you can do is prune to a downward-facing side branch on that branch, continuing the outward growth but with a small kink. This produces an interesting look halfway between a goblet and a fully flat pollard, and is also a great way to extend an established pollard in the future.

....

OPPOSITE, TOP: **Pollarded planes for sale at NV Solitair nursery, Belgium.** Photo by NV Solitair.
OPPOSITE, BOTTOM, LEFT: **A young tree being trained into a parasol form.** Photo by Laura Knosp.
OPPOSITE, BOTTOM, RIGHT: **Winter pruning of a young pollarded lime: one of the easiest, most satisfying garden jobs out there.**
PAGE 148–149: **These lime drumsticks make up for lack of a canopy with excessive epicormic growth.**

Pollards come in all shapes and sizes

of them. Two is not enough for a pollard, but if you have too many, thin out those that are too close together, leaving a well-spaced arrangement. Choose a diameter of about 5 ft. (1.5 m) for the tree, so the branches should grow to roughly 30 in. (75 cm) from the trunk—as they reach that mark, cut them back.

Of course, not all pollards are wide spreading—some are tall and thin, with side branches running the whole way down the trunk. The Japanese prune their street trees like this, notably the ginkgos.

As a gardener, you should assess the situation at the end of the growing season, or the next spring if you would like to keep the recent growth on over the winter. You might decide that you left too many side branches, and now is the time to remove a couple more. Prune away all the new growth, apart from the main branches (not forgetting to leave any in-fillers you might have selected). This will seem a significant step backwards, but in time, the core structure of the trunk and branches will develop enough to have its own winter presence.

The next few years are the same: more formative work, developing and defining the structure of the tree. As with all pruning jobs, a pollard is never really finished—each year will be better than the last, and you always

know that the next year will be better still. Pruning for ornamental pollards ought to be a yearly job, but it is not the end of the world if you miss a year—just carry on as you would have the year before, cutting right back to the tree's original framework.

In my opinion, pollards really come into their own in winter, and ideally should be pruned soon after leaf fall to accentuate their sculptural qualities in the winter light. In areas where they are grown as shade trees, pruning at the start of winter also lets in more light when it is needed, but with willows and some limes, this removes the interesting bark colours too early for some people's liking. Each to their own—when it comes to regular pruning, pollarding is one of the easiest, most satisfying garden jobs out there. Very little thought is needed, just a sharp pair of secateurs (or a machete) and occasionally a pruning saw. When cutting off all the season's growth, go right back to the base. As it is new growth, only just turned woody, it will be lovely and soft, buttery almost—removing this is one of my favourite autumn jobs.

In time, your frame will develop the lovely, knobbly bolls of swollen cambium that give pollards their character. A feature of some established pollards are the vertical, club-like stalagmites found either halfway down or at the end of branches. These occur where short lengths of vertical growth have been allowed to remain, intentionally or otherwise. There is no single style for an ornamental pollard—they can be flat, goblet-shaped, or a mixture of the two, they can have wide branches, no branches at all, there can be lots of side branches, just a few, and there can even be knobbly bits if you want.

If you have an established tree and would like to create a pollard on a more ambitious scale, apart from needing a chainsaw and a set of ladders, there is not very much difference in approach. Reduce the tree down to the selected set of side branches, then the resulting new growth down to the desired number and spacing, and continue with regular pruning from then on. This is a great way of managing a large tree. Although it might look drastic for the first year, it will soon start to develop a new character.

If you have really caught the pollarding bug and feel the need to plant an entire avenue, use the pruned shoots for cutting material—I have had great success with replanting plane cuttings in the past. The advantage of using your own cuttings is that you know what you are getting, and they should all be identical clones, important if you are planting a formal avenue. Needless to say, only take cuttings from a tree with a good form and habit—we have a pair of young pollarded limes that have noticeably different growth habits—one is more vigorous and upright, the other more messy. Had I known this at the start, I would have looked for two of the vigorous, upright ones, which unsurprisingly seems to produce a better pollard than the messy one.

Willow pollards

Another great raw material for European pollarding, especially further north, is the willow. Large, pollarded willows are a common sight along rivers throughout northern Europe, their squat trunks making dark silhouettes in the winter months. The larger trees are either *Salix alba* (white willow) or *Salix fragilis* (crack willow) although as Archie Miles points out in his book *Silva*, the two are hard to tell apart and hybridize enthusiastically anyway.

In the wetlands of Somerset, in the south west of England, *osiers* (French for willows, from the Latin *osera*) are known as withies. Coppicing is often used on these instead of pollarding as a more efficient method of production for basket making. The coppicing is done entirely by machine, much like a combine harvester, giving a decidedly agricultural feel to things. Traditional basket making in this area has been in decline since the introduction of plastics, but recent trends have helped the industry recover, with biodegradable willow coffins becoming a popular new line.

Ornamentally, willow varieties are ideally suited to pollarding, partly because the colour of the new growth's bark is accentuated, and is strongest during its first year. They are also quick growers, able to establish a good, shaggy head of growth on top of a trunk in one season. In northern Europe, pollarded willows are used in gardens much as formal standard trees are. Cut back annually, they provide a strong, sculptural presence over the winter and bushy foliage over the summer, but beyond their physical presence, they are also a reference to the landscape and culture of the local *osier* production.

Lucien den Arend is an environmental artist whose work often involves pollarded willows. Born in Holland, much of his work is site-specific, landscape-based sculpture. He uses pollards in large grid formations, such as at the Pieter Janszoon Saenredam Project in Barendrecht, The Netherlands, seeking a connection between modernist symmetry and the traditional uses of willow trees. In a rectangular reservoir built within a new housing project, den Arend built a square island, planted with 256 willows in a grid formation, echoing the willow-lined canals of the Dutch lowlands. As with the plane trees at the City Hall in San Francisco, I am attracted to the juxtaposition of 'man' and 'nature' in den Arend's work—the rigidity of the grid system, the

natural and organic trees growing within it, and the human intervention of pruning that brings the trees back a step closer to man. Gardening, for me, is a fascinating balancing act between garden and gardener—and the more contradictions involved and subtleties touched upon in this relationship, the better.

COPPICING

Coppicing, like pollarding, is a woodsman's craft. Its basic principle is very similar to pollarding—that of regular cutting back of all growth—except rather than cutting to the trunk, coppices are cut right back, almost to ground level. Pollarding for short people. As previously mentioned, the withy beds of Somerset are coppiced, as are sweet chestnuts (*Castanea sativa*) in the south of England. Their steel-grey poles are harvested for hurdling and fencing on a 15-year cycle. Chestnut wood splits easily, so it is easy to process, as well as being rich in tannins, giving it a long life. Hazel coppice (*Corylus avellana*) is grown in a similar way, but coppiced more frequently, over a 5–7 year cycle. In Japan, evergreens such as *Lithocarpus edulis*, *Castanopsis cuspidata*, *Quercus phillyreoides*, and other oaks are coppiced in areas known as *satoyama*, the marginal woodlands that border rural villages. I have a pair of shears whose handles come from coppiced *Quercus myrsinifolia* that was produced in just such a location. As in the UK, these environments went into decline in the twentieth century, but are now valued for their biodiversity. Elsewhere, holm oak (*Quercus ilex*) in the south of France and teak (*Tectona grandis*) in the tropics are coppiced in a similar manner.

....

PAGE 152-153: **Willow pollards adding a sense of character to the landscape.**
PAGE 154, TOP: **Harvested willow, Somerset.**
PAGE 154, BOTTOM: **Lucien den Arend's Janszoon Saenredam Project, Barendrecht, The Netherlands.** Photo by Lucien den Arend.
PAGE 155: **Pruned and unpruned pollards in Belgium.**
OPPOSITE: **Bring a touch of the woods into the garden with coppiced hazels and snowdrops.**

Out of the woods and into the garden, coppicing plays a less obvious role than pollarding, but not only is it a useful way of controlling the size of a tree, it is a great way of capturing some woodland atmosphere. From an ecological point of view, coppices are home to a wide range of wildlife—their dense growth provides a safe habitat for small mammals by raising them just off the ground, away from predators. Not only that, because the trees are constantly changing, growing and being cut back, they are home to a wider range of fauna than might be found on other trees, as they cast less shade so a wider variety of flora can grow around them. Visually, the old stumps of coppices, the stools, soon gather moss and develop a character all of their own, adding that sense of maturity and stillness that woodland trees have.

Regular coppicing also brings out the best in some plants. Many willows (species of *Salix*) and dogwoods (species of *Cornus*) reward hard pruning with brightly coloured and attractive bark on new growth, while trees like *Paulownia tomentosa* regenerate with such vigor after being cut back that their new leaves can be more than 2 ft. (60 cm) across, providing a striking foliage effect that can reach 10 ft. (3 m) or more in one summer.

Of course, when coppicing is only done once, or very occasionally in a tree's life, it really amounts to a multi-stemmed tree. Nurseries in Japan produce trees in just this way—evergreens such as *Quercus myrsinifolia*, *Ilex pedunculosa* and deciduous *Styrax japonicus*, *Cornus kousa* and *Acer palmatum* are cut right back to the ground at the nursery, much like coppicing. The new growth is then allowed to mature into a multi-stemmed tree that can be thinned and pruned when in situ in the garden.

RAISING

Following on from the production of multi-stemmed trees, comes this most satisfying of pruning jobs—raising, or lifting the crown, which reveals the trunk or branch structure beneath the canopy of the tree. A

visit to a Belgian nursery, Solitair, and an introduction to their basic philosophy that plants can be improved upon by subtle pruning just as much as by severe clipping or shaping, demonstrates the virtues of this most sculptural of techniques.

At Solitair, rows and rows of evergreen shrubs such as *Osmanthus ×burkwoodii* and various rhododendrons lie in different stages of production, their tops clipped into shape and their lower branches removed to show off their interesting branch structure. When buying in or growing on stock, special care is taken to select interesting, multi-stemmed plants that might otherwise have been ignored, as their trunk patterns create the most interesting results. Nearby were rows of box tables: box rectangles that had had their lower branches removed, but the twist this time were the flat slabs on top. All they needed were miniature chairs and tea sets to complete them.

Tom Stuart-Smith also raised the trunks of some *Viburnum rhytidophyllum* in his 2006 RHS Chelsea gold medal garden. The viburnums' raised, spidery trunks were silhouetted against rich ochre walls, providing stunning reflections in the geometric planes of water present in the garden. Nurseries like Architectural Plants in West Sussex, England, are also up to all sorts of similar techniques to improve the look of

a plant. The basic premise is very Japanese—the insistence that, without drastically changing a plant, a sharp pair of secateurs and a few decisive gestures can make all the difference. The great thing about it is how rapidly one gets results, with no waiting around for years and years, patiently hoping that next year will be the one when everything comes to fruition. Within five minutes or so, all the work is done, and the results (good or bad) are plain to see.

Revealing multi-stems

Conifers and evergreens are the obvious candidates for this treatment, as they give year-round interest, but it is worth remembering that deciduous shrubs can look great in the winter as well, especially those with an interesting trunk pattern or a clipped top. Whatever one uses, the basic approach is the same. Start with an established shrub, the bushier the better. The difference between a shrub and a tree can at times be quite vague, but in this case it is straightforward: we want a bushy, multi-stemmed plant, rather than a single-trunked one, so even a tree such as *Quercus ilex* would be a good subject, despite its potential size, providing it is multi-stemmed.

A quick word of warning: this is an easy job but does involve a bit of hands and knees work. You'll also need a good pair of secateurs and perhaps a small pruning saw (the Japanese-style pull saws are easier to use than Western-style push saws in this kind of situation.)

Knowing when to stop is the crucial part of this job. Often it is obvious, with the plant suggesting a natural pause through its growth habit or flushes of branches. Other times it is less clear, but think about stopping roughly a third of the way up the trunk to start with— you can always come back to it after lunch. This job is really a two-parter, the bottom and the top. Like all good jobs, it can be split further into endless possibilities, depending on the plant you started with and the end result you have in mind, but the basic question to ask yourself as regards the top half is: to prune or

OPPOSITE, TOP: **Coppiced sweet chestnut (***Castanea sativa***) provides the perfect habitat for blue bells.**
OPPOSITE, BOTTOM, LEFT: **Coppiced *Paulownia tomentosa* puts on close to 10 ft. (3 m) of growth the following year, with vast leaves.**
OPPOSITE, BOTTOM, RIGHT: **Multi-stemmed *Quercus myrsinifolia* in Japan.**
PAGE 160, TOP: **Raised rhododendrons at Solitair.** Photo by NV Solitair.
PAGE 160, BOTTOM: **Box tables at Solitair.** Photo by NV Solitair.
PAGE 161, TOP: **A well-raised example of *Pinus densiflora* 'Umbraculifera' in Tokyo, Japan.**
PAGE 161, BOTTOM: **Espaliered Gala apple trees and winding box hedges combined with raised, multi-stemmed hornbeams (*Carpinus betulus* 'Fastigiata') in this garden by Joseph Hillenmeyer in Kentucky, U.S.A.** Photo by J. Hillenmeyer.

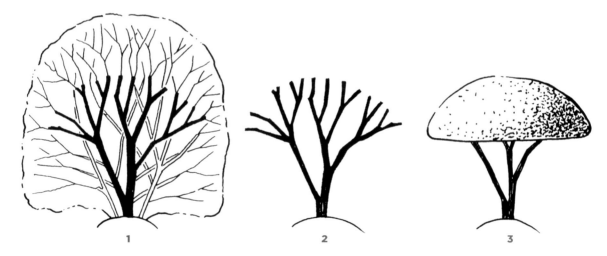

1. Examine the shrub, decide if it has a front (if it is planted in the ground, then you obviously have less choice) and look at the branch structure. In your head, try to reduce the main stems down to the strongest few, following them from the ground up.

2. With these main stems in mind, start removing the lowest, superfluous side branches. Some of these could be potential keepers, so go slow. Step back every few minutes—or have someone behind you (preferably someone you are prepared to listen to) offering advice. Next, look at whether you need to remove any of the main stems themselves, to lighten and thin the structure. Often stems will fork low down, and removing one half will enhance the other—in this case you usually want to remove the inward-facing of the two, to encourage a good wide shape.

3. Prune the top of the shrub into a rounded, clipped head if desired.

not to prune? A pruned top can complete the sculptural process, but in some cases is not appropriate and a free-growing look might be more suitable. In that case, then there is no more pruning to do, but if you would like more definition, then some sort of pruning is necessary.

Plants like *Osmanthus ×burkwoodii*, with its small, evergreen leaves, respond very well to clipping and look fantastic made into parachutes or umbrellas. If you started with a dome or egg shape, then there is now little more to do than regular clipping each year, but if you want to make a parachute shape, go over the top with a pair of shears. Finally, spend a few minutes tidying up the edges and underside. Remove any bits on the stems that you might have missed and go around the outside, around the equator, making the line between the two hemispheres as tight and clean as possible. In the future, watch out for epicormic growth cluttering up the clean structure of the stems and clip the top as much as you feel necessary.

Experiments like these are common enough in many nurseries and gardens, but seeing them in whole rows, in their hundreds, gives more conviction and an added sense of gravitas to the idea, suggesting endless possibilities to gardeners with a less spectacular scale to work in. Everyone has an old shrub at the back of a bor-

OPPOSITE, TOP PHOTOS: **Removing just a few of the lowest branches of this *Myrtus apiculata* reveals the attractive bark and gives it the presence of a small tree, not a shrub.**
OPPOSITE, BOTTOM: **Raising the crown has been taken to its logical conclusion on these *Ficus microcarpa* in San Francisco, U.S.A.**

der, just sitting there waiting for enlightenment, or a gloomy corner that has become overgrown or impenetrable and is ripe for some decisive action. Removing the lower branches of an overgrown shrub is just about the easiest thing possible, instantly adding a sculptural presence as well as letting in light below and reclaiming valuable space.

Having discussed pollarding, coppicing and raising, we are now perfectly poised to look at my favourite of all trees, the Japanese *daisugi* or *kitayama sugi: Cryptomeria japonica* var. *radicans*. Combining various elements of tree pruning, this conifer is traditionally grown in the Kitayama region, north of Kyoto, as a forestry crop, where the trunk is cut a few feet from the ground and, unlike most conifers, sends out new shoots from the old wood, which are then thinned to a handful of new, vertical leaders. As these new leaders grow, their lower side branches are removed, every year or two, resulting in a very pure, knot-less timber which is used as a traditional house building material. When the trunks reach a suitable size, they are cut, allowing new ones up in their place. These forestry techniques were adopted into domestic gardens (I have heard that the Emperor was in the Kitayama area one day and was so impressed by the trees that he asked to have them in his garden—a nice story, but no doubt overly simplified and I have no idea which Emperor), resulting in a remarkable style of tree unique to the Kansai area around Kyoto, a sort of raised coppice on a rotation system, giving the impression of a clump of trees, but all stemming from the same trunk. For me, these trees epitomize Kyoto gardens even more than the pines do, with their squat bases, tall, thin trunks and fresh, green growth on top.

FRUIT

Welcome to the murky world of fruit pruning, with its delights, pitfalls, curious terminology like stepover and oblique cordon, pruning techniques such as the modified Lorette system, and rootstocks that sound like road names. I must admit to having little technical knowledge or experience of fruit tree pruning prior to researching this book, but on closer inspection, two things have become apparent: firstly, it is easier than it looks, and secondly, it is not that different to other pruning techniques used in the garden.

Action is reaction

During my investigations, I spent a cold, damp, but very interesting February afternoon with Cor van Oorschot, the orchard manager at Blackmoor Estate in Hampshire, who talked me through the key processes involved in commercial fruit growing. He showed me some basic stuff—the difference between a flower bud and a leaf bud (the flower buds are fatter and rounder than the leaf ones, becoming more obvious towards the end of winter when they start to swell) and also explained the importance of each year's growth. He pointed out that certain methods were based around nursery economics, where yield has to be balanced with efficiency, but that in the garden, things can be done slightly differently, with equal emphasis on ornament and yield.

The overall lesson I came away with that day, Cor's mantra, was that "Action is Reaction." Everything one does to a plant has a result, therefore every action causes a reaction. By this, he meant that deliberate cuts (or tears—Cor does a lot of pruning with his bare hands, claiming that by ripping the wood rather than cutting it, he does less damage to the cell structure, helping the plant to avoid disease) inevitably cause a series of consequential events that in turn need to be dealt with through more pruning. The same could be said about most of the pruning techniques in this book, where one action leads to another, which in turn leads to another,

OPPOSITE, TOP PHOTOS: **Cor van Oorschot demonstrating where to prune to encourage more horizontal growth.**
OPPOSITE, BOTTOM, LEFT: **Commercial pruning is not always pretty—branch stubs are deliberately left to encourage new shoots for the future.**
OPPOSITE, BOTTOM, RIGHT: **A similar branch, one year later.**

and so on—but somehow, hearing it with a Dutch accent gives it more resonance.

A lot of time is spent in the orchards at Blackmoor encouraging the trees to grow less and fruit more. Pruning is the main tool used here, but ironically the very action of pruning provokes the tree into yet more growth, which in turn will need thinning and removing. Heavily pruned trees are also root pruned to check the new growth that the pruning encourages—in this process, a large blade is dragged along the roots of the rows of the trees like a plough, cutting the roots on two sides just enough to disturb the trees, without actually harming them. Every job requires another after it in the pursuit of fruit—Cor's mantra.

Most commercial apple orchards in the UK now grow the majority of their produce on a style of tree known as the spindle. This is a narrow, feathered tree with a single leader that produces fruit on its side branches. Different varieties need slightly different pruning and spacing—Gala, for example, produce fruit on first, second and third year growth, whereas Braeburn produce it only on second and third year growth. Pruning encourages the well spaced, horizontal side branches that bear the fruit. Overcrowded areas are thinned to allow light in to the fruit, but the branches are cut back to stubs, rather than flush with the trunk, so that they send out new shoots, which in time will replace older side branches, in a constant cycle of fruit-bearing material.

The Lorette system

Originally, apple and pear pruning was a winter job, but a Frenchman, Louis Lorette, introduced the idea that summer pruning produced a better yield. His technique involved pruning back new growth as it turned woody, in three monthly sessions over the summer, to encourage fruit to grow within the structure of the tree. While working in a cooler climate in England in 1934, A. H. Lees simplified the Lorette system to just one summer prune, usually in August—hence the modified Lorette system in use today. Coupled with pruning out older

wood in winter, this is the fundamental pruning practice regarding apples and pears in temperate climates today.

Ornamental fruit training

If one senses a danger of becoming too immersed in the technical side of fruit growing, I suggest a visit to your nearest kitchen gardens to see how it can be done productively *and* ornamentally. A favourite of mine is West Dean gardens in Sussex, England, where head gardener Jim Buckland and his wife, Sarah Wain, oversee the beautiful walled gardens there that are packed to the brim with trained fruit trees, vegetables and glass houses.

Training is the name of the game at West Dean: diagonal and double cordons, espaliers, tunnels, four-winged pyramids, goblets, fan training and free-standing trees—the list goes on. What struck me, on a recent spring visit, was actually how simple it all looked. With no foliage to hide the structure of the trees, it was clear that for all their fancy names, these different styles all depended on the same basic principles that the commercial growers use, albeit with rather more style: encourage horizontal or diagonal branches, let enough light in, and reduce leafy growth. Of course, reducing it down like that completely glosses over the skill, care and passion involved at West Dean. It looks simple, because it is done so well.

The training of branches, or the entire tree in the case of the cordon, helps slow down growth and encourages fruiting instead. It also makes the best use of space, keeps things within reach, and crucially, is where the ornamental opportunities creep in. From an aesthetic, sculptural point of view, there are direct comparisons to be made between fruit training and ornamental garden training. The espalier, for example, appears to be no different to a pleached hedge, except perhaps in scale. When used along a path, it even serves a similar purpose. The low trunk of the single tier espalier (often known as a stepover due to its height) also bears a strong

resemblance to the extended branches of pine trees in Japanese gardens, as they are trained out along paths and supported on crutches. The technique is known as *katanagareshitate* (a bit of a mouthful which roughly translates as extending branches) and examples of it can run for dozens of feet away from the tree itself. Then there is the training of individual branches of standard fruit trees—the intentions may differ, but in real terms the effects are very similar to those of many Japanese *niwaki*.

As a creative exercise, it is fun to imagine further crossover potential with ornamental fruit in the garden. The traditional, walled kitchen garden is based around a formal layout of paths and beds, but what if fruit trees were planted in the garden in a more natural manner, creating a sense of landscape like Japanese gardens do? Having a small orchard at the end of a garden goes some way towards this—the character of old apples would add a real sense of maturity to the garden—but taking the idea further, there could be single branches of apple trees sneaking across the lawn, a fusion of the stepover and *katanagareshitate* techniques. Alternatively, how about fan-trained Japanese pines?

The wall-trained espalier is another good bridging example—*Pyracantha* is the obvious choice, but a more interesting idea is the *Ginkgo biloba* at the National Arboretum in Washington D.C., U.S.A. This is not a tree one expects to see clinging to a wall, nor, in the Western world, is it one that is pruned much at all (you must head off to Japan to learn about ginkgo pruning), but thinking about it, it seems a fantastic choice for this treatment—the natural growth of the ginkgo, with its straight branches studded with foliage, is unlike any other tree, and would be perfectly suited to the espalier.

Thinking out loud like this, playing around with possibilities and hypothetical ideas, reaffirms my belief that all creative, imaginative pruning boils down to the same thing, regardless of scale, setting or species. Topiary, fruit, *niwaki*, tree pruning, even agricultural pruning are all ultimately just an extension of the individual at work in the garden. The terminology is all well and good in defining and describing what we do, but it is the end result that counts. "It ain't your sign, it's your mind," as Roy Ayers once sang.

....

PAGE 167: **Peach fan, West Dean, Sussex. England.**
PAGE 168, COUNTERCLOCKWISE: **Espaliered apple tree (in England) and trained fig tree (in Japan) share similar techniques with Japanese pine training—the bottom branch of this black pine runs barely 6 in. (15 cm) above the ground.**
PAGE 169, TOP AND BOTTOM, LEFT: **This espaliered apple tree and *Podocarpus macrophyllus* share certain qualitites. Top photo by Graham B. Bould.**
PAGE 169, BOTTOM, RIGHT: **Espaliered *Ginkgo biloba* at the National Arboretum, Washington D.C., U.S.A. Photo by Chris Mann.**
OPPOSITE: **Pear cordon, West Dean, Sussex, England.**

SIX
Creative Pruning Close to Home

DECORATIVE TREE PRUNING and creative topiary exists in various guises all over the world: in the centuries-old traditions of formal European topiary, in the garden trees of the Far East, in the streets of San Francisco, and in the magical realist world of Zarcero in Costa Rica. The most interesting examples of these are found in gardens that, to me at least, do not subscribe to one particular style—-ones that do not specifically declare themselves as topiary gardens, Japanese gardens or architectural gardens, but rather include elements from whatever takes their owners' fancy.

HARVARD FARM

For obvious reasons, I am particularly fond of my parents' home in Dorset, Harvard Farm, in the south west of England. The garden was started from scratch in 1992, so it has only begun to reach maturity in the last few years. It is an informal, family garden, with a large trampoline parked firmly in the middle of the lawn throughout the year. Its foundations are the ragstone walls of the original farmyard, to which new retaining and ornamental walls were added, linking the garden to its surrounding Dorset landscape, as the ragstone itself was dug out of the heavy clay soil from under the garden—literally prized out with a crowbar, in some cases. Within the garden's walls is what appears to be a quintessentially English garden: two lawns, borders, a spring wildflower meadow area, an apple tunnel, steps and terraces, and an enormous range of planting, all on

a relaxed, informal scale. Bringing it all together, however, is a generous use of evergreens that were planted not just for their winter foliage, but also to establish some cover on the windy, hilltop site.

It is these evergreens that we are interested in here. Like all gardeners faced with an empty plot and an eager enthusiasm, Mum overplanted. As the plants finally got going, there was the inevitable natural selection process, as the losers were gradually weeded out, but still there was too much for the garden. Mum knew that she wanted strong, clipped shapes, but it just so happened that I came back from my spell in Japan at exactly the time that these evergreens needed some serious attention. *Phillyrea latifolia, Quercus ilex, Osmanthus ×burkwoodii, Laurus nobilis, Ilex aquifolium, Elaeagnus ×ebbingei, Lonicera nitida*, of course *Buxus sempervirens*, and various other conifers, notably *Taxus baccata* and species of *Cupressus*. These had all finally become established in the heavy clay soil and strong winds, and were busily blocking pathways and crowding out other plants. My suggestion was to incorporate some of what I had learned in Japan into the garden, experimenting with Japanese techniques on these decidedly un-Japanese plants.

The results, we think, work very well. Some shapes are clearly Japanese in style, others are less intentional and more organic, but what they all do is fit into the garden as a landscape. Deliberately *niwaki*-styled *Phillyrea latifolia* sit at crucial points on the corners of buildings. A row of yew *twmps* evolved almost accidentally out of a hedge that refused to cooperate, as some plants in the row struggled to establish themselves in our stony clay. Large, bloated *Elaeagnus ×ebbingei* kidneys frame views onto the lawn and down towards the *twmps*, like bladders ready to burst. *Buxus sempervirens* shapes are dotted about the border, no two alike. Come winter, with the garden reduced to its bare bones, these shapes assume a new importance. Where in mid summer, their role is to offer a contrast to the rich, varied planting around them, in the winter they take centre stage, particularly on clear frosty mornings in the low, winter light.

The clipping process is now shared out among everyone available. I started most projects, but have moved away since then. My father, an artist, adds his own perspective to things when he gets going. Rob, the gardener, does more than anyone, and Mum, busy with the borders, takes care of the smaller jobs. Timing is based on manpower and necessity rather than a well-planned policy. Family events and open days during the summer mean things sometimes get clipped earlier or later than perhaps they should, but in a family garden that is how it works.

At every turn in the garden, strong, organic shapes provide structure, framing views, adding definition to the planting schemes and linking the garden with the landscape beyond: the rolling hills and hedgerows of the Dorset countryside. Despite the amount of clipping that goes on, Mum is adamant that this is no topiary garden, but what it proves is that there is room in almost any garden for a bit of creative pruning. It can be light hearted and fun without being tacky, and it can be clever and sophisticated without being cold and detached. Crucially, it fits in without being overpowering, adding character and an extra element to the garden without dominating it.

The view of the drive, seen from the front door, shows how clipped shapes and evergreens interact well with foliage and color. Some shapes, such as the *Phillyrea lat-*

OPPOSITE: **Harvard Farm.**

ifolia niwaki, are kept tight and well clipped throughout the year, while others, such as the *Rhamnus alaternus* pyramid are only clipped once a year, allowing the edges to blur. Weeping willow, *Eriobotrya japonica*, variegated evergreen and deciduous *Elaeagnus*, a red *Prunus*, roses, even yuccas, and the young ash plantation behind, all act as a foil for the strongly clipped shapes in the foreground.

It is interesting to compare this view of the drive with that of one of my favourite gardens in Kyoto, the temple of Konchi-in—not because our garden, not yet 20 years old, could possibly compare with one of the more important temple gardens in Kyoto, built over 400 years ago, but because elements of it are remarkably similar. The basic physical layout and topography is very alike: the flat foreground, the bank and taller trees behind. Of course, the temple gravel gets raked each morning, and has no cars turning on it, but what both pictures show is that strong, clipped shapes can interact well with the mixture of foliage, colour and texture, adding a sense of focus and depth.

The Japanese-style *Phillyrea latifolia* are a particular feature of the garden, and work well against the stone farmhouse and outbuildings. *Phillyrea* is a great choice for this sort of pruning as its foliage is dense, evergreen and relatively small. They get clipped twice a year, once in early summer (quite a hard clip, cutting right back to the original outlines, to keep the branches from getting too big) and then again at the end of the summer, usually sometime in September. As with all evergreens, they drop a lot of old yellow leaves in the early summer, just when they are putting on their growth spurt, so it pays to give them a good shake when pruning, to

....

encourage them off—there is nothing worse than having a good pruning session, tidying up and then the next day seeing more mess from fallen leaves.

Between the terrace and the top lawn, a low, worm-like *Lonicera nitida* hedge merges into a larger thorn hedge, adding to the informal feel of the garden and creating lovely gateways to two pathways and steps down to the terrace. *Lonicera* is a fantastic option if you want fast results for a hedge, but it grows amazingly quickly and fairly messily—it needs constant pruning and once established, benefits from clipping at least once a month through late spring to early autumn. Frankly, I have better things to do with my time than tending to it.

The apple tunnel, inspired by the one at Heale House in Wiltshire, England, consists of a steel frame and a collection of favourite apples trained over the arches and espaliered along wires. The apples cover the entire season, from Discovery right up to Jonagold, and get pruned twice a year—the woody growth is thinned over the winter and the soft growth cut back mid summer to help the fruit to ripen. Both sides of the tunnel are flanked by rows of irregular *Buxus sempervirens* shapes. They are intentionally not perfect balls, but lumpy, organic things that create a softer, more relaxed feel–and are much easier to clip. They get dealt with just once a year, clipped with an electric hedge trimmer in early summer.

The border, meanwhile, is packed full of colour and foliage, as well as a few large standards (*Laurus nobilis* and *Pittosporum tenuifolium*) that are raised above the level of the herbaceous plants. One bay is being cloud pruned, bit-by-bit. It stared off as a predictable, bushy, egg shape, but was taking up too much valuable space. Rather than raising it into a standard lollipop or mushroom (the obvious solution, but we already had two standards in the border), we decided to give it a more Japanese look and it has proven to be successful material for this kind of treatment—even though because of its vigour and the size of its leaves, each branch needs to be on a fairly large scale. Using Japanese techniques on

a plant so strongly associated with the Mediterranean might seem like a contradiction, but then the English garden has never been the place to worry about dilemmas like that and it certainly does not bother us.

Various green and variegated box is scattered throughout the front of the border, in random shapes that have suggested themselves over the years: irregular spirals and helter-skelters, strange ball-on-cube-on-plinth shapes and cones that have slowly morphed into teardrops, so much so that they now resemble fat penguins. They are all placed towards the front of the border, and in the summer their role constantly changes as the plants around them grow and flower. Their early summer clip sharpens them, bringing them into focus and adding their distinct outlines that in turn give a sense of depth to the border they sit in. Over the course of the summer they lose their edge, putting on that slightly annoying second flush of growth that fails to grow evenly all over, appearing instead in patches of light green. A few minutes with a pair of shears puts an end to this, bringing things back into focus, but nevertheless an autumn clip freshens everything up for the winter.

Around the back of the large barn, which is used as a painting studio by my father, lurk yet more surprises. A pair of *Cupressus arizonica* var. *glabra* flank the doors to the barn, clipped into very deliberate Japanese *tamazukuri* forms. They started off life as typical conifer shapes, and over three or four years were clipped and shaped until they reached their finished condition.

....

PAGE 180: *Cupressus arizonica* var. *glabra tamazukuri* outside the barn.
PAGE 181: **View of the terrace with the apple tunnel in the foreground.**
OPPOSITE, TOP TWO PHOTOS: **The instantly recognisable outline of *Pinus pinea* in San Francisco, U.S.A. and Rome, Italy (photo by Marion Slawson).**
OPPOSITE, BOTTOM TWO PHOTOS: *Pinus pinea*, **before and after. The results are bolder and more sculptural. There is also room to walk past the tree now, and it is no longer growing into the yew hedge behind it.**

The yew *twmps* opposite them are the result of a less than successful hedge. Young plants were planted in what is basically reclaimed, heavily compressed clay soil—not the best start for any plants, let alone yew. Over the years they got established, but never in a uniform manner that suggested a formal hedge, so as much out of impatience as anything else, we started clipping individual plants. They are at their best seen obliquely, especially on a frosty winter morning. The advantage of this irregular style, beyond its visual strengths, is that weaker plants can be pruned into smaller shapes or removed altogether, without upsetting the balance of things. Nor do mistakes through heavy-handed pruning stand out as strongly as in formal hedges, and uncertainties can always be ironed out later on.

The garden was designed to create different areas, and views, at every turn. From the lawns, glimpses of views offer themselves in all directions, usually defined by the topiary—the sharp outline of clipped box balls against the house, peeking out from under the shade of a fig tree, or the random arrangement of cones and domes on the terrace (bay, *Elaeagnus* and *Phillyrea*) like the roofscape of a Renaissance town. A pair of small *Phillyrea* trees sitting in the corner of the lower lawn have somehow escaped pruning altogether. One day something will be done about them, but for now they exist in their natural form, overseeing all around them.

ARCHITECTURAL PLANTS

The term architectural has become part of the horticultural language over the past 20 years or so. The expression was coined by Angus White, and it was his nursery, Architectural Plants, in Sussex, England, that led the way in defining its parameters. In his brochure, Angus describes plants as architectural "not because they belong in buildings, but because the plants themselves have their own 'architecture'—strong, sometimes spectacular, shapes which bring a distinctive year-round presence to the garden." This includes "Spiky, Frondy, Palmy, Bold, Outrageous, Adventurous, Exciting, Dra-

matic, Theatrical, Spectacular, Preposterous, Tropical-Looking and Larger Than Life" plants such as palms, ferns, bamboos, yuccas and bananas, but it also covers plants that can have architecture "thrust upon them"—the trees and shrubs that respond well to a bit of creative tweaking. This is the bit that I find interesting, the bit where nature provides the raw materials for us to interpret in our own individual ways.

The nursery at Architectural Plants is centred around the office and sales area, and is flanked by the garden where they practise what they preach, experimenting boldly and stretching common horticultural practices well beyond their usual boundaries. If I describe the place with too much enthusiasm then please forgive me—I used to work there, and have many fond memories.

In the woodland valley garden, a canopy of native trees, mostly oak and ash, have had their crowns lifted to create a clear area for the exotic planting. The canopy above protects the more tender plants below from the worst of the frost, and visually it creates a striking landscape, especially when seen from the jetty which overlooks the valley: the tall, clear trunks are at eye level, with lush, green exotics below. Tree ferns, *Trachycarpus* palms, unusual conifers such as *Podocarpus salignus*, evergreen shrubs like *Hebe parviflora* and a range of bamboos give the place a decidedly exotic feel.

What the staff at Architectural Plants do is help plants on their way. They present evergreen trees as just that—trees. Their trunks are grown straight and their foliage is pruned to give the impression of what the tree will look like in its mature state. In the garden and stock field, larger specimens of these trees can be found, showing what one could expect a young tree to turn into over the years. Nothing is left to chance here—once young trees have been established, the trunks are raised and, depending on the species, the crowns are pruned to keep them at a manageable height and to create a denser, more rounded head. Angus describes the look

as Carmel, referring to the slick look of the California coast, where evergreens are often clipped into umbrella and mushroom shapes.

Plants with interesting bark tend to get the raised crown or multi-stemmed treatment, to show off the bark as much as possible. Orange barked myrtle (*Myrtus apiculata*) Santa Cruz ironwood (*Lyonothamnus floribundus* subsp. *aspleniifolius)* and the Jounama snow gum (*Eucalyptus pauciflora* subsp. *debeuzevillei)* are obvious candidates. They even go so far as to peel the bark from the ironwood trunks to reveal a fresh layer below, speeding up a natural process to enhance the overall look, squeezing out every last drop of potential.

The tree that one nearly always sees with a deliberately raised crown, and falls neatly into the architectural stable, is the Italian pine, *Pinus pinea*. Whether dotted across the landscapes of Italy, the streets of San Francisco, or the Home Counties of England, their distinct, mushroom-like outline is instantly recognisable. In the garden, *Pinus pinea* benefits from pruning for two reasons: to enhance its characteristic mushroom shape that naturally develops as the tree gets bigger, and to tidy up the look of the tree—the lower branches soon lose their needles in the shade, starting to look spindly and untidy, so removing a whorl of branches every year or two (as new flushes produce new whorls at the top) kills two birds with one stone.

Pruning the lower branches from pines is even more straightforward than other trees, as they grow in such regular whorls, one flush each year, that the process involved is pretty simple: saw an entire whorl off (usually 3-5 branches). Step back and have a look. Repeat if necessary. Knowing when to stop is the key, but even then, should you have taken off more than was wise, it will only be a year or so before the new growth on top will redress the balance.

....

OPPOSITE: **Cut larger branches in two stages.**

184

Removing large branches of any tree should be done in two stages. First, remove the weight of the branch by sawing 12 in. (30 cm) or so from the trunk. Then cut the stub off smoothly, at the collar (the swollen ring around the branch where it meets the trunk). This prevents the bark tearing from the weight of the branch during the pruning, and is a good practice to follow when making any cut.

Now is a good time to point out, or revisit, how trees and shrubs grow: from the top, not the bottom. The buds at the ends of every branch are where the following year's growth stems from. It is obvious when one stops to think about it, and it is why low branches on a tree will remain where they are—they will not rise up the trunk each year as the tree gets taller. So the trunk of Italian pines (or any tree) will not stretch magically like a worm being pulled from the ground by a bird. If you want a longer trunk, chopping off the lower branches is the only way.

Not all these techniques are rocket science, and Angus White and his gang are the first to admit it, but to be successful they have to be done well, with enthusiasm and conviction—the conviction that what you are doing is right, and that it will improve the look of the plant in your garden. The belief that we are able to improve upon something as naturally beautiful as the tree is essential. Not everyone agrees of course (not that it matters—they will have probably thrown down this book in fury long ago) but it is vital to remember that we are working within the confines of a garden (not the wilderness) which, despite being full of plants, is a man-made environment. It is our intervention that created it in the first place, and our creative curiosity that gives it life and continues to expand it.

Taking the notion of thrusting architecture on plants a bit further, Architectural Plants also produce their own Japanese-style *niwaki*. The European market is flooded with imported *Ilex crenata* nowadays (in the UK and most of Europe, they come from Italian nurseries who have imported them from Japan) and they have become synonymous with the terms *niwaki* or cloud tree, but in Japan the *Ilex crenata* is one of the most very basic garden trees, the poor man's *niwaki*. It is never used in temple gardens, where the pine (primarily *Pinus thunbergii* and *densiflora*) is king, and in private gardens it is reserved for secondary roles. Think of it as privet.

So, it is quite exciting to see Japanese principles applied to something a bit different, in this case *Phillyrea latifolia* and *Myrtus apiculata*. Both plants add something unusual to the mix, in a way that *Ilex crenata* never does: the myrtle has its flaky bark, which comes off to reveal a downy, warm orange under-layer. It also flowers profusely, however hard you prune it (believe me—I have tried). *Phillyrea* brings a quality all of its own to pruning projects; its rich green foliage is dark and glossy, the bark, in time, grey and textured, not unlike that of a box tree, only darker. It trains and clips extremely well (as does the myrtle) and is one of the very best plants for a range of topiary.

It is interesting to notice that these and other techniques that seem so radical and exciting are perfectly normal practices in other parts of the world. Japanese gardeners might be interested in *Myrtus apiculata* as a plant, perhaps having not seen it before (traditionally Japanese gardens use a very limited palette of native plants) but they would not bat an eyelid at its trained and pruned appearance.

Another shape popular at Architectural Plants is the blob. The nursery is full of them, in all sizes and species: yew, box, Japanese holly, evergreen azalea— you name it. In the garden, virtually everything is fair game to be blobbed—*Choisya ternata*, *Hebe parviflora*, *Euonymus japonicus*, whatever takes their fancy. Very much inspired by Japanese azalea *karikomi*, these blobs are natural, organic shapes—mushrooms with-

....

OPPOSITE: **Machu Picchu meets West Sussex, with *Butia capitata*. Photo by Angus White, Architectural Plants.**
PAGE 188: **Stripped trachies. Photo by Angus White, Architectural Plants.**

out stems. Angus calls their kind of clipping shaping rather than topiary, to distinguish it from the traditional interpretation.

They even give bamboo the blob treatment, in particular the lower growing spreaders such as *Pleioblastus pygmaeus* 'Distichus'. Left to its own devices, it makes a great ground cover, gobbling up bare ground and nutrients wherever it spreads, but here it is clipped, with shears, into shape. In Japan, it is generally clipped (or even strimmed) into contour-hugging drifts, but in the shade of the eucalyptus trees at Architectural Plants, the shapes of the bamboo are more three-dimensional, more sculptural, more Machu Picchu. Colin, the gardener responsible for so much that goes on in this garden, clips throughout the summer, treating the bamboo as what it is, a member of the grass family. Little and often is the name of the game, as cutting bamboos back too deep results in lots of bare canes with no foliage. Of course, the good thing about bamboo is that should one make a real mess, the following year there will be a whole new flush of material to work on.

They get up to other techniques at Architectural Plants too, some that do not necessarily fall into the creative pruning category, but that involve the use of sharp blades and a creative eye nevertheless: yuccas, cordylines and palms are brown bitted—where the older, browning foliage at the bottom of plants is removed, leaving only the fresher, greener flush at the top. Much like raising the crown of a tree, this not only gets rid of the messy bits, but also gives the plant more of a trunk (or at least reveals it), giving it more stature and presence. More radical stuff goes on too, such as stripping trachies, which involves removing the hairy fibres from *Trachycarpus fortunei* with a bread knife to reveal the hard trunk beneath, a beautiful, creamy coloured trunk that dries to a rich chestnut brown. The result is striking, and not as unnatural as one might think, as in time the hairy fibres drop off anyway, albeit not quite as dramatically as this, so in effect it is merely accelerating the natural process, with added intensity.

Much of the inspiration for Angus's enthusiasm for pruning comes from the Mediterranean, where the boundaries between pruning, topiary and other work in the garden have always been less clearly defined. A walk around most Italian or Provençal towns demonstrates the fact that pruning is an important tool which plays a strong role in defining the Mediterranean look. From enormous, pollarded street trees, to rows of oleander standards lining shopping streets, the evergreen *Magnolia grandiflora* and *Ligustrum delavayanum* topiary and of course the fruit trees, pruning is everywhere one looks.

Pinus pinea and *Cupressus sempervirens*, those two most Mediterranean of trees, pop up constantly in this landscape, in the towns and in gardens. I describe the pair as being self-pruning trees, because when left to their own devices, they eventually manifest themselves as very strongly defined, sculptural trees. The true form of *Cupressus sempervirens* results in a surprisingly solid-looking shape in its native environment, eventually filling out to become quite wide, while the commonly available 'Stricta' or 'Fastigiata' variety has been bred to retain its columnar form on a much smaller scale. Despite this breeding, the pencil thin cypresses can very quickly lose their shape if not clipped regularly, especially in milder, wetter climates. Much as with fastigiate yews (*Taxus baccata* 'Fastigiata'), the side growth of cypresses can sometimes be so vigorous that its own weight drags it down, peeling itself away from the body of the tree. If ignored, this side growth quickly fills out and the form of the tree is lost within a few years.

The solution to bloated cypress trees, needless to say, is pruning. A story Angus White tells, which illustrates the case for pruning so vividly, is when on a trip to a large nursery in the Pistoia region of Italy, he asked how they managed to get their cypress trees looking so good. The answer came not in words, but in the simple gesture of wielding a pair of shears. Clipping cypress trees in the garden is the only way of keeping them reliably tight and columnar, especially if their height is being

checked. Fortunately, it is a straightforward job, save for a stiff neck and the inevitable clippings down one's shirt.

Cypresses do not re-sprout willingly from old wood, so the secret is to keep on top of things and clip more than once each year—ideally two or even three times until late summer. Use hedge shears and work vertically, up and down the tree. I find it helps to keep your body close to the tree, to get a better feel for the surface. At the point where you switch from clipping upwards to downwards, watch out for the divide, taking care to clip evenly the whole way down.

In time, especially nearer the top, the woody growth will get thicker and thicker, and there becomes a danger of losing the shape, which can be a problem if you want the pointy look. Heavy shearing will keep this problem at bay, but over time you will end up with bare woody patches with no foliage on. To prevent this—and prevent it you must—use secateurs to cut out the thickest growth, cutting back inside the foliage. This might leave the odd hole in the short-term, but that will soon grow in with soft new foliage and be much more manageable in future.

Clipping in the summer, you will also find your shears clog up with the oily resin of the foliage. This is unavoidable, and can become a real bore, as more and more effort is needed to open the blades after each cut. As with box clipping, one solution is to have a bucket of water handy and stick the blades in every so often, to wash the resin off. Or put your waterproofs on and clip in the rain, as wet foliage achieves the same result. After all, if you have made it all the way through this book, a bit of rain will not hurt.

....

OPPOSITE, LEFT AND TOP RIGHT: *Cupressus sempervirens* as they should be, in a customer's garden, and as they should not be, in a nursery in Italy. Photos by Angus White, Architectural Plants.
OPPOSITE, BOTTOM, RIGHT: The terraced gardens of Gordes, France, are defined by neatly clipped *Cupressus sempervirens*.

CONCLUSION

TO CONCLUDE with the same point I made in the preface, in pruning everything is interconnected. Hedges, topiary, pleaching, pollarding, *niwaki*—it all boils down to the same thing, and it relies on an inquisitive mind and a creative approach to lift it above the mundane and into something extraordinary.

Where pruning might go from here is an interesting question—trends change, but for every decline there follows a revival. The influence of the East will surely continue to grow, along with an informal style of pruning that embraces natural, organic forms. Conversely, formal topiary and traditional western skills will continue to thrive as people refine, and redefine, them. Who knows, perhaps my ideas about guerilla pruning will catch on? Whatever happens, I hope that my thoughts inspire you and make you look at things in a new light, and that the next time you head out into the garden, you are clutching something sharp. Good luck and happy pruning.

OPPOSITE: **Getty Museum, California, U.S.A.** Photo by Scott Woodruff.

REFERENCES

Ardery, Julie, "Evergreen Surrealist—Pearl Fryer", *Human Flower Project*. http://humanflowerproject. com/index.php/weblog/comments/ evergreen_surrealist_pearl_fryar/.

Clevely, A. M., *Topiary*. London: Collins, 1998.

Dagley, J. R. and Burman, P, "The Management of the Pollards of Epping Forest", quoted in Read, Helen J. (ed), *Pollard and Veteran Tree Management II*. London: Richmond Publishing and the Corporation of London, 1996.

Daponte, R., Forestry Commision, "New Forest Fact File", *Open Forest: Ancient and Ornamental Woodlands and their Management*, http://www. forestry.gov.uk/pdf/AncientOrnamentalwoodland. pdf/$FILE/AncientOrnamentalwoodland.pdf.

Dufour, Annie-Hélène, *L'arbre familier en Provence*. Aix-en-Provence: Edisud, 2001.

Hillier Nurseries, *The Hillier Manual of Trees & Shrubs*, pocket ed. Newton Abbot: David & Charles, 1998.

Hirahara, Naomi, *Green Makers: Japanese-American Gardeners in Southern California*. Los Angeles: Southern California Gardeners' Federation, 2000. Joyce, David, *Pruning & Training Plants*. London: Mitchell Beazley, 1992.

Marqueyssac information leaflet, *Les Jardins Suspendus de Marqueyssac*.

Miles, Archie, *Silva: British Trees*. London, Ebury Press, 1999.

Oedo-Botania, *Oedo-Botania*, http://www. oedobotania.com.

Sullivan, Mike, *The Trees of San Francisco*. Petaluma: Pomegranate Communications Inc., 2004.

White, Angus, *Architectural Plants: The Nineteenth Impression*. Catalogue, 2009.

Yamada, Shoji and Hartman, Earl (trans), *Shots in the Dark*. Chicago: University of Chicago Press, 2009.

Yama-Kei Publishers, *Nihon no Jyumoku* [Woody Plants of Japan]. Tokyo: Yama-Kei Publishers, 1985.

OPPOSITE: **Jacques Wirtz's garden.**

ACKNOWLEDGEMENTS

MANY THANKS TO EVERYONE who very kindly contributed photographs to this project. Unfortunately I was unable to personally visit all of the examples of pruning featured in this book, but I have been fortunate enough to be able to benefit from the generosity of the following photographers, gardeners, artists and institutions: Lucien den Arend, Nic Barlow, Danny Beath, Michael Bell, Lars K. at Solsken Design, Graham Bould, Graeme Churchard, David Davis, Brian Eden, Peter Edwards, Mark Fountain, Jeffrey Friedl, Jan Geerts, J S Gim, Yves Gosse de Gorre, Rob Harrison, Charles Hawes, Maria Hiles, Joseph Hillenmeyer, Robert Ketchell, Ted Kipping at Tree Shapers, Laura Knosp, Beatrice Krehl, Daniel Ladd, Roy Lathwell, Jean Laugery, Jacinta Lluch, Chris Mann, David Martinez, James Mitchell, Didier Morlot, Nagasaki University Library, David Nash, Lesley Powell, Alex Ramsay, Marion Slawson, Kent Smith, Solitair Nursery, Edzard Teubert, Yasuhito Tobitsuka, Angus White and Scott Woodruff.

I am also grateful to the following for their inspiration, encouragement and information, and especially to those who opened their doors—or gates—to me: Jim Buckland at West Dean, Noi Rittirat, Peter Sievert, Sir Michael Butler, Rosemary Alexander, John and Jenny Makepeace, Marqueyssac, Angus White at Architectural Plants, The European Boxwood and Topiary Society, Mark Bourne, Blackmoor Estate, Solitair Nursery, the Harley Estate, The Pearl Fryar Topiary Garden, Wirtz International, Levens Hall, Nicky Fraser, Heale House, the Rebdis and Joseph Hillenmeyer.

....

OPPOSITE: **Pearl Fryar's garden.** Photo by Nic Barlow.

INDEX

Pages in boldface include photographs or illustrations.